Spinoza's *Ethics*

Indiana Philosophical Guides

Spinoza's *Ethics*

Beth Lord

Indiana University Press
Bloomington and Indianapolis

This book is a publication of

Indiana University Press
601 North Morton Street
Bloomington, Indiana 47404-3797 USA

www.iupress.indiana.edu

Telephone orders	800-842-6796
Fax orders	812-855-7931
Orders by e-mail	iuporder@indiana.edu

First published in the United Kingdom by
Edinburgh University Press

Typeset in 11/13 pt. Monotype Baskerville by
Servis Filmsetting Ltd., Stockport, Cheshire

Manufactured in Great Britain

Cataloging information is available from the Library of Congress.

ISBN 978-0-253-35484-6 (cl.)
ISBN 978-0-253-22204-6 (pbk.)

1 2 3 4 5 15 14 13 12 11 10

Contents

Series Editor's Preface

To us, the principle of this series of books is clear and simple: what readers new to philosophical classics need first and foremost is help with *reading* these key texts. That is to say, help with the often antique or artificial style, the twists and turns of arguments on the page, as well as the vocabulary found in many philosophical works. New readers also need help with those first few daunting and disorienting sections of these books, the point of which are not at all obvious. The books in this series take you through each text step-by-step, explaining complex key terms and difficult passages which help to illustrate the way a philosopher thinks in prose.

We have designed each volume in the series to correspond to the way the texts are actually taught at universities around the world, and have included helpful guidance on writing university-level essays or examination answers. Designed to be read alongside the text, our aim is to enable you to *read* philosophical texts with confidence and perception. This will enable you to make your own judgements on the texts, and on the variety of opinions to be found concerning them. We want you to feel able to join the great dialogue of philosophy, rather than remain a well-informed eavesdropper.

Douglas Burnham

Acknowledgements

I thank all my colleagues at the University of Dundee, who have given me the opportunity to teach Spinoza and much support in writing this book. Thanks are due to series editor, Douglas Burnham, and to the editorial staff at Edinburgh University Press, for helpful comments along the way. I thank my husband, Jim Tomlinson, for his help and support. Above all, I wish to thank the students to whom I have taught Spinoza over the past five years. Their ideas, questions and ways of understanding and failing to understand Spinoza gave this book its shape. I especially thank the class of 2008, on whom many of the ideas in this book were tested.

List of Figures

For Jim, who is full of joy.

Introduction

Why Read this Book?

This is a guidebook to the *Ethics*, the major work of the seventeenth-century philosopher Baruch Spinoza. This book differs from other introductory books on Spinoza in a number of ways. First, it does not assume that you have any philosophical background. I do not presume that you know (or remember) Descartes' theory of substance, that you understand what 'extension' means or that you already know what 'naturalism' is. As far as possible, I explain Spinoza in terms that any reader can understand. Second, this book is designed to be read alongside the *Ethics*, page by page. I imagine you have both books open in front of you, turning to this book for clarification after reading a few pages of Spinoza. You will find concepts explained in exactly the same order as they arise in the *Ethics*. You can work through the book systematically or turn to specific sections as you need them.

Most importantly, this is a guide to *reading* the *Ethics*. It is not a guide to the critical literature, scholarly disagreements or objections of other philosophers. There are plenty of good books that will introduce you to those things. The belief guiding *this* book is that you need to read the text for yourself before getting embroiled in analysis and critical discussion. This book focuses on the *Ethics* itself. As you will see, I hardly make reference to critics and commentators at all.[1] Nor do I spend much time on those problems in the *Ethics* that are

---

[1]   That is not to say that I have not made use of other commentators. Hallett (1957), Hampshire (1987), Curley (1988), and Deleuze (1988) have particularly influenced my interpretation of Spinoza. For historical material I have drawn especially on Israel (2001), and Nadler (2001).

entrenched as major scholarly debates. Instead, I consider the questions and problems that you, the reader, are likely to come up with and that generally go unanswered in philosophy books. These are the kinds of questions that my students find most compelling: How does Spinoza account for disability? What does his ethics say about animals? Is anger always evil? Is every aspect of my future already determined?

In short, this book is an explication of Spinoza's *Ethics*. Any explication of a text involves interpretation: choices about which topics to emphasise, how to understand key terms and sometimes, which of a variety of 'traditions' of reading Spinoza to follow. In this book, I have tried as far as possible to leave those traditions to one side and to offer an original interpretation of Spinoza based on reading the text itself. As you gain confidence in reading, your interpretation may differ from mine. All the better: this is a workbook for reading and understanding the *Ethics*. It is also a prompt for raising your own philosophical questions about the text and about the world.

Why Read Spinoza's *Ethics*?

Why are *you* reading Spinoza's *Ethics*? Perhaps it is assigned reading on a university course. Maybe you are a philosopher who wants to brush up on a neglected area. Or perhaps you are led by curiosity about the nature of reality, the mind and human behaviour. If you fall into any of these categories, this book – and indeed, Spinoza's *Ethics* itself – was written for you.

It may surprise you to hear that Spinoza's *Ethics* was written just as much for a non-expert audience in the twenty-first century as for the philosophical world of the seventeenth. Spinoza anticipated that his book would be read largely by those steeped in the philosophical traditions of the time. (If you do have some philosophical background, you may hear echoes of Plato, Aristotle, the Stoics, Descartes and Hobbes in his work, as well as anticipations of Nietzsche, Sartre, Foucault and Deleuze.) But Spinoza would be delighted to learn of non-experts reading his work more than 300 years later, for his aim is to help as many people as possible understand the truth. The *Ethics* is a workbook designed to enable the reader to develop his or her own understanding. Spinoza thinks that if more people read the *Ethics*, then reason and virtue amongst human beings will increase, leading to more peaceful and tolerant societies.

That is not to say that the *Ethics* is a kind of early self-help manual. Spinoza's *Ethics* is a rich and complex work of metaphysics, epistemology and ethics. Undoubtedly, it is one of the most difficult philosophical books you will ever read. You will grapple with language and concepts that are unfamiliar and encounter ideas with which you may disagree profoundly. But it is also one of the most exciting philosophy books ever written. Spinoza gives us a programme for being human beings in the best way possible – a programme based on a deep understanding of the nature of reality that anyone can attain. He leads us on a journey that reveals to us the truth about what we are and our place in the universe. Understanding the truth about ourselves is the basis for positive human relationships, true scientific knowledge and good political organisation.

Spinoza can lead you to think differently about yourself and your life, about nature, about God, about freedom and about ethics. So perhaps the best reason for reading Spinoza's *Ethics* is this: it is a book that may change your life.

Spinoza: Rationalist, Empiricist, Atheist, Radical?

Spinoza (1632–77) is a philosopher of the seventeenth century. If you are a philosophy student, you may already know something about seventeenth-century philosophy from reading Descartes or Hobbes. You may know about eighteenth-century philosophy from reading Hume, Kant or Rousseau. Philosophers of this era have certain interests in common:

- the necessary existence of God;
- the nature of experience;
- the nature of substances;
- the role of reason in knowledge;
- the relation between mind and body;
- the question of freedom.

According to their views on these subjects, philosophers of the seventeenth and eighteenth centuries are divided into categories. Are they rationalists or empiricists about knowledge? Are they materialists or idealists about reality? Typically, Spinoza is cast as a rationalist and a materialist: someone who believes that reason is the main ingredient of our knowledge of a world that is exclusively material.

These distinctions are not very helpful. Spinoza is called a rationalist because of the centrality of rational knowledge to his system. But if we call him a rationalist, we lose sight of the enormous emphasis he places on the experience and capabilities of the body. While Spinoza believes that the truth is known through reason, he also believes that rational knowledge could not be attained without experience and experiments. It is one of the aims of this book to persuade you that Spinoza is just as much an empiricist as he is a rationalist.

Another label frequently applied to Spinoza is 'atheist'. This may surprise you when you start to read the *Ethics*, since its first part is dedicated to proving the existence and nature of God. Spinoza is indeed an 'atheist' insofar as he denies the existence of the God of theism – an anthropomorphic, intentional God to be feared, worshipped and obeyed. Spinoza's dismissal of the theistic idea of God as illusory led him to be castigated as one who denies God altogether. However, it is clear that Spinoza believes very strongly in God in a different sense: a God that is identical with nature. This has led him to be labelled a pantheist (someone who believes God is everywhere) and a panentheist (someone who believes God is in every being).

Categorising Spinoza along these lines is useful only to the extent that it reminds us of the uniqueness of his system. Spinoza is interested in the same questions that other philosophers of his era were writing about, but he approaches them in a very different way. Spinoza is radical in his metaphysics, epistemology and ethics. The word 'radical' refers both to Spinoza's distinctness from the philosophical mainstream and to his subversion of it. Spinoza actively undermined establishment views about philosophy, religion and politics, because he believed that his society had got all three badly wrong. Spinoza's philosophical radicalism therefore runs parallel to his religious and political radicalism, for which he would be punished with exile, censorship and vilification.

Who was Spinoza?

Spinoza was born in Amsterdam in 1632, in the midst of an explosion of scientific, artistic and intellectual discoveries. The same decade saw the birth of John Locke, Louis XIV and Isaac Newton. In Amsterdam in 1632–3, Rembrandt van Rijn was painting the works that would establish him as a great artist and René Descartes was preparing to write his first philosophical works. In London, William Harvey had recently published his discoveries on the circulation of the blood, while in Florence, Galileo Galilei was placed under house arrest for defending the view that the earth revolves around the sun.

Bento, Baruch or Benedict de Spinoza was the son of Portuguese Jews who had fled religious persecution in Portugal at the end of the 1500s. (Bento, Spinoza's Portuguese name, was translated as Baruch in Hebrew – meaning 'blessed' – and Benedict in Latin.) Jews were persecuted throughout Europe at this time. Those countries that would accept them did not grant them full citizenship or rights to participate in the local economy, and often did not allow them to practise their religion. They were subject to prejudice, hatred and violence from the Christian authorities. In countries such as Spain and Portugal, Jews were obliged to convert (outwardly, at least) to Catholicism in order to avoid expulsion. These converts were known as marranos, and they lived as refugees even in the countries in which they were born.

When the Spinoza family emigrated to Amsterdam, it was to a comparatively tolerant society. Although Jews were not granted full rights of citizenship, they were allowed to run businesses, and made a major contribution to the economic success of the city. They were also allowed to practise Judaism openly, as long as the community regulated itself closely and did not interfere with the Christian majority. It was in this community of settled refugees that the Spinoza family ran a merchant business, importing wine, olive oil and other goods from Portugal.

The Dutch Republic in the 1650s and 1660s was economically very powerful. It was the wealthiest nation in Europe, largely due to its control of trade networks between Europe and Asia. A republic since the late sixteenth century, it was one of the first 'modern' states, for its strength lay in capitalism rather than the absolute power of a monarch or the wealth of an aristocracy. Its governance, however, was highly unstable. For much of Spinoza's adult life, the Republic was led by a liberal republican, Jan de Witt, and governed and administered by wealthy merchants and their companies. But a major political faction, aligned with the Calvinist Church, supported the return of quasi-monarchical power to the House of Orange, and eventually seized power and assassinated de Witt in 1672. Throughout these decades, members of liberal and radical factions who publicly called for greater democracy and religious and economic reform risked censorship, imprisonment and exile. Meanwhile, the Dutch Republic was embroiled in a succession of wars with England and France.

Spinoza attended a Jewish school, learning Hebrew, theology, and commerce, to prepare him to work in his father's business, which he did until the age of 23. But his interests lay elsewhere, and he sought help from Franciscus van den Enden, a former Jesuit who taught Spinoza Latin and introduced him to the philosophy of Descartes. He very likely introduced Spinoza to radical politics as well. Beyond this, Spinoza had no formal philosophical training.

At the age of 23, in 1656, Spinoza was expelled from the Jewish community. Nobody is entirely certain why. The proclamation of expulsion refers to 'evil opinions and acts' and 'abominable heresies which he practised and taught'. Spinoza may have circulated unorthodox views about God or established an unsanctioned theological discussion group. It is certain that he had ties with political liberals outside the Jewish community. The Jewish authorities knew that toleration of Jews in Amsterdam rested on the contribution of Jewish merchants to the city's economy. They knew, too, that the rights they enjoyed could easily be taken away. If any individual Jew criticised the Dutch political or religious establishment, or questioned the way the Jewish community regulated itself, he put the entire community at risk. Expulsion was the most extreme sanction the Jewish religious authorities could impose on such a person. And unlike most other expulsions of the time, Spinoza's was permanent. Whatever danger Spinoza posed, exclusion was perceived to be the only way of dispelling it.

Spinoza's expulsion is not to be understood as an 'excommunication' in the way that term is used in the Catholic Church. For the Jewish community, which lacked the power of statehood, expulsion was one of a limited number of ways of maintaining discipline. Individuals who did not conform to the religious, social or ethical norms of the community could be punished only by withholding rights to take part in certain community activities. These activities were deeply embedded in the Jewish way of life and their deprivation was life-diminishing (Nadler 2001: 4).

Whether or not Spinoza's offence did strike at the economic, political and religious stability of the community, his punishment deprived him of political, economic and religious status. He was banished from the Amsterdam community and from the family business, and was instead forced to live elsewhere and had to make his own way in the world. Despite its difficulties, this must have been just what Spinoza wanted: he was free to turn his back on the mercantile life and focus on philosophy, and now found a new community amongst the intellectuals, political radicals and religious dissenters of Leiden and the Hague. He learned the craft of lens-making, and was able to make a modest living grinding lenses for spectacles and microscopes until he died of lung disease (probably as a result of inhaling glass filaments) at the age of 45. Lens-making was a particularly appropriate activity for a philosopher who sought to enable people to see reality with greater clarity and distinctness.

In some ways, Spinoza had the archetypal existence of the reclusive philosopher: he lived alone, never married, never owned property and distanced himself from everyday material concerns. But Spinoza believed strongly in the power of communities, and maintained contact with local and international circles of philosophers and freethinkers. His life was exactly the striving for greater rationality and virtue that his philosophy recommends to others.

Spinoza's Works

During his lifetime, Spinoza published just two works: *Principles of Cartesian Philosophy and Metaphysical Thoughts* (1663) and the *Theological-Political Treatise* (1670). His other texts, *The Treatise on the Emendation of the Intellect*, the *Short Treatise on God, Man, and his Wellbeing*, the *Hebrew Grammar* and the unfinished *Political Treatise* were published, along with the *Ethics*, by Spinoza's followers after his death.

The reason for the delayed publication of the *Ethics* was the reputation Spinoza had acquired as a result of the *Theological-Political Treatise*. This work is a religious and political critique directly responsive to the Dutch Republic in the 1660s. It combines a critical study of the Bible with a critique of religious authority and a defence of liberal democracy, tolerance and freedom of expression. To say that the *Theological-Political Treatise* is radical is an understatement. Spinoza set out to demolish the whole system of established beliefs about political and religious authority, provoking condemnation and violent opposition. As one historian puts it:

> In the entire history of modern thought, only Marx and Nietzsche have so openly and provocatively repudiated almost the entire belief-system of the society around them, as Spinoza does here. (Israel 2001: 220)

To understand why Spinoza caused such outrage, read the following passage from his Preface to the *Theological-Political Treatise*:

> I have often wondered that men who make a boast of professing the Christian religion, which is a religion of love, joy, peace, temperance and honest dealing with all men, should quarrel so fiercely and display the bitterest hatred towards one another day by day . . .. I am quite certain that it stems from a widespread popular attitude of mind which looks on the ministries of the Church as dignities, its offices as posts of emolument and its pastors as eminent personages. For as soon as the Church's true function began to be thus distorted, every worthless fellow felt an intense desire to enter holy orders . . .. Little wonder then, . . . that faith has become identical with credulity and biased dogma. But what dogma! Degrading rational man to beast, completely inhibiting man's free judgment and his capacity to distinguish true from false, and apparently devised with the set purpose of utterly extinguishing the light of reason. Piety and religion . . . take the form of ridiculous mysteries, and men who utterly despise reason, who reject and turn away from the intellect as naturally corrupt – these are the men (and this is of all things the most iniquitous) who are believed to possess the divine light! (TPT Pref., CW 390–1)

Spinoza's criticism is breathtaking, even today. He accuses the Church of appointing self-aggrandising, anti-intellectual fools to positions of authority and of guiding people through lies and deceit. Religious dogma prevents people from using their reason, while faith is nothing more than superstition that inhibits enlightenment.

Organised religion is anti-rational and leads to hatred, violence and war.

Spinoza wants to diagnose *why* people irrationally follow such systems. Why, he wonders, are people distracted from Christianity's message of joy and love towards hatred and resentment? Why do they put up with a government that leads them into endless wars? And why do the majority long for *less* freedom and tolerance by fighting for the return of a monarch? Spinoza's answer is that both Church and State encourage the masses to remain irrational and powerless, thus ensuring the continuance of their own power. The result is a society of people discouraged from using their reason, who not only tolerate their own enslavement but actively fight for it.

Enlightenment involves enabling people to make use of their own reason. But Spinoza recognises that increased rationality depends on a change in political and social conditions. A liberal democracy, freedom of expression and the rejection of superstition are necessary conditions for the free use of reason. Spinoza argues that the Bible is not the word of God revealing metaphysical truths, but a human text, subject to critical interpretation like any other work of literature. A miracle is not a divine intervention, but a natural event whose causes are unknown to us. Theology is therefore distinct from philosophy and the sciences, and total freedom of expression should be allowed in the latter. The civil state can flourish and fulfil its purpose – greater freedom – only if people are free to exercise their reason.

The *Theological-Political Treatise* was published anonymously, but Spinoza quickly became known as its author. The result was explosive: he was charged with atheism, sacrilege and denial of the soul, and was attacked by all sides of the religious and philosophical spectrum. Spinoza became known throughout Europe as the dangerous and subversive author of a book that was universally banned.

This led to the widespread vilification of Spinoza's thought, but also to underground currents of interest from free-thinkers all over Europe. 'Spinozist' became a term of derision and shorthand for a variety of anti-establishment positions; it was used as an insult and threat to anyone propounding ideas even slightly related to Spinoza's. Throughout the eighteenth and nineteenth centuries, the accusation of 'Spinozism' led philosophers to be dismissed from their posts and their books to be banned. So feared was this accusation that it became commonplace for philosophers to publish denunciations of Spinoza – in most cases, without ever having read his work! It was not until the 1780s that it became acceptable to read his works, and even then, it was not without a *frisson* of danger.

The public outcry against the *Theological-Political Treatise* made it impossible for Spinoza to publish his major work, the *Ethics,* during his lifetime. When it was published after his death in 1677, it too was banned. However, Spinoza was able to send drafts to his friends and followers. The 'Spinozist circle' was in regular correspondence with Spinoza and wrote to him often, seeking clarification of some of his more obscure points. We have them to thank for some of Spinoza's clearest explanations and for giving us some indication of Spinoza's personality. Like any teacher, Spinoza is happy to offer his help – but only to students who genuinely make the effort to learn.

Writing and Reading the *Ethics*

One reason for the difficulty of reading the *Ethics* is that Spinoza wrote it using 'the geometrical method'. The *Ethics* is not written in paragraphs of fluent prose, but in definitions, axioms, propositions and demonstrations.

Why does Spinoza use the geometrical method, which he himself admits is 'cumbersome'? Setting out propositions geometrically was not a wholly uncommon mode of philosophical presentation at the time. It enables the philosopher to construct a grid of cross-references, each proposition demonstrable by reference to earlier ones, building up to a complex network of interrelated truths. Many students, once they get used to it, actually prefer Spinoza's geometrical method to the florid prose of Hume or the awkward textual constructions of Kant. Every proposition is fully explained, right there and then. If you cannot understand how a proposition is justified, Spinoza tells you exactly which earlier propositions you need to return to in order to demonstrate it. It is a remarkably clear and efficient method of writing.

Spinoza has another good reason for using the geometrical method, namely, that it has an important relation to the way the reader's understanding develops. Earlier, I called the *Ethics* a workbook designed to help the reader develop his or her own reasoning.

The *Ethics* is therefore not like philosophical texts written in prose. It is not a commentary on reality that explains the truth. Rather, it is an exercise in *unfolding* the truth through the *active thinking* of the reader. The *Ethics* is philosophy as activity and performance. As we read it, we are meant to be caught up in a certain movement of thought and to understand the truth through the activity that Spinoza draws us into. The reader is displaced from her usual position of externality to the text and made to be part of its workings. This is one reason why the *Ethics* is so difficult to read, but also why it is so intoxicating.

The revelation of truth through the reader's thinking activity reflects Spinoza's belief (which we will discuss further in Part II) that a true idea is an activity of thought. A true idea is not a picture in the mind and it cannot adequately be expressed using representational means, such as language or pictures. That means that a text – any text – will be inadequate with respect to true ideas. A text can symbolically *represent* those true ideas, and the best texts will prompt us to *actively think* true ideas. Spinoza's text, then, does not tell you the truth as a narrative. It aims to engage you in active thinking, to know the truth for yourself and thus to build your own rational understanding (Deleuze 1988: 83). This is best achieved through the geometrical method, which requires the reader to understand ideas as they follow logically from other ideas. For Spinoza, this logical order is the order of true understanding, as we shall see in Part I. As we perform each demonstration, our own thinking latches on to that order of true understanding.

In the *Ethics*, you will encounter the following elements:

- **Definitions** which set out the meanings of key terms.
- **Axioms** which set out basic, self-evident truths. (More will be said about definitions and axioms in Part I.)
- **Propositions** – the points that Spinoza argues for – and their **demonstrations**.
- **Corollaries**, which are propositions that follow directly from the propositions they are appended to.
- **Lemma**: propositions specifically related to physical bodies (these appear only in Part II).
- **Postulates**: assumptions about the human body that are drawn from (and apparently, justified by) common experience.

- **Scholia**: explanatory remarks on the propositions. In the scholia, Spinoza comments on his demonstrations, gives examples, raises and replies to objections and makes piquant observations about people's beliefs and practices. The scholia are some of the most interesting and enjoyable passages of the *Ethics*.

Before we begin, here are a few tips for reading the *Ethics*:

- It is important to read the book sequentially. Because the later propositions depend on earlier ones, this is not a book in which you can easily skip back and forth.
- If time allows, read the whole of the *Ethics*. If your university course treats only some sections of the text, read the whole Part in which those sections occur.
- Read slowly and carefully. Try to understand what Spinoza is trying to prove and to work through Spinoza's demonstration.
- Sometimes it is helpful to read over a few propositions quickly, to get a gist of where Spinoza is going, before returning to read the demonstrations and scholia in detail.
- You may need to read some demonstrations multiple times (and even then, they may not make sense).
- You will encounter a lot of terms that are unfamiliar or that don't mean what you think they mean. Don't panic – this book is here to help.

Make use of this *Philosophical Guide* to whatever extent you find helpful. It can be read concurrently with the *Ethics* or referred to afterwards. I clarify Spinoza's meaning as I understand it, based on my extensive work with his text and commentaries on it. I offer relevant examples as often as possible. I have developed a series of figures which illustrate some of Spinoza's most difficult points. My concern throughout has been with the experience of you, the reader, as you encounter the difficulties of the *Ethics*, and as you discover its fascination.

Abbreviations

I refer to Edwin Curley's translation of the *Ethics*. Quotes and other references are not to page number, but rather to proposition number (and, where relevant, corollary number, scholium number, etc.). I make use of the following abbreviations.

D = Definition
A = Axiom
P = Proposition
Dem. = Demonstration
C = Corollary
S = Scholium
Exp. = Explanation
L = Lemma
Post. = Postulate
Pref. = Preface
App. = Appendix
Def. Aff. = 'Definitions of the Affects' at the end of Part III.

Each section of this book looks at one Part of the *Ethics*. When I refer to material from that Part within its designated section, I simply note the proposition number (for example: D3 = Definition 3; P33S = Proposition 33, Scholium; P16C2 = Proposition 16, Corollary 2). When I refer to material from another Part, the Part number is given in roman numerals (ID5 = Part I, Definition 5; IIL7 = Part II, Lemma 7; IVP37S2 = Part IV, Proposition 37, Scholium 2).

Occasionally I refer to Spinoza's other works:

TEI (followed by paragraph number) = *Treatise on the Emendation of the Intellect*

TPT = *Theological-Political Treatise*

Letter (followed by letter number) = an item from Spinoza's correspondence

CW = Spinoza's *Complete Works*, translated by Samuel Shirley.

1. A Guide to the Text

Part I: Being, Substance, God, Nature

Probably the most difficult challenge you will face in reading the *Ethics* is getting through Part I. You are presented with strange terminology, difficult metaphysical concepts and a series of arguments that don't seem to be about anything real or concrete. These barriers can make reading this Part confusing, frustrating and boring. But with a little guidance, these initial sections will open up and become clearer. Once you have grasped the basic ideas Spinoza sets out, you will begin to understand his conception of reality, and that gives you the key to everything else in the book. The aim of this section is to help you to read this first Part and to clarify your own understanding – not only of Spinoza's text, but of reality itself.

One of the reasons for the difficulty of Part I is that it is concerned with ontology. Ontology is the theory of being: before we understand what *things* are, we need to understand what *being* is. What are we talking about when we say that things *are*? What is the source of the *being* of things? Even trying to think about these questions is difficult, let alone trying to answer them. You may wonder why it is important to answer these questions, given that our knowledge and experience is of concrete *things*, not of abstract *being as such*. Spinoza believes that we need to start with *being* because *being* is not a conceptual abstraction; it is the concrete ground of all of reality. Only once we understand what *being* is will we have the right basis for understanding objects, people, ideas and the universe.

Spinoza's basic idea is that *being is one*, that *being* is equivalent to God and that all the individual beings we experience are 'modes' of being and thus 'modes' of God. This is what Spinoza tries to convince you of in Part I.

The Seventeenth-century Common-sense View

One way in to the *Ethics* is to consider the readers for whom Spinoza was writing. Seventeenth-century readers came to Spinoza's text with a certain common-sense view of the world, a view which Spinoza hoped to convince them was misguided. Taking their perspective helps us to understand his purpose; at the same time, it makes us question the common-sense views that we too bring to the text. This helpful method of starting to read the *Ethics* I borrow from Curley (1988).

Spinoza knew that his readers would come to the *Ethics* with some ontological ideas already in mind. This is no less true today than it was in the seventeenth century. Even if you don't have a well worked-out theory of being, it is inevitable that you hold *some* conception of reality. It is likely, for instance, that you think of the things in the world around you as separate, individual objects. Probably you think of yourself as something that is independent of material things and different from them due to your subjectivity, consciousness or free will. Perhaps you think of your mind as a wholly material part of the body, or perhaps that your mind is a different, immaterial kind of entity. You may think of yourself as having a soul that will exist in another form after death.

Spinoza's seventeenth-century readership would have held a similar set of views, a combination of the Aristotelian principles that had been the basis of science and metaphysics for hundreds of years, and the philosophy of minds and bodies that had recently been proposed by Descartes. Spinoza's readers were thoroughly familiar with certain Aristotelian principles, the most basic of which is the idea that the universe is made up of substances and their attributes. For Aristotle, substances are the basic, independently existing 'things' of the universe, and attributes are their changeable properties. Whereas attributes depend on substances for their existence, substances do not *logically* depend on anything beyond themselves. The existence of a substance, such as a human body, does not *logically require* the existence of anything else to be what it is. By contrast, the property 'weight' cannot exist unless it is the weight of some body. 'Weight' does not exist independently; it *logically requires* the existence of a substance in order to exist.

Descartes heavily revised this Aristotelian picture in his 1644 work *Principles of Philosophy* and in his earlier *Meditations on First Philosophy*. The ideas in these texts shook up the Aristotelian world-view which had held sway for centuries. Descartes agreed with Aristotle that the universe is made up of innumerable substances with changeable properties. But he believed that underlying those changeable properties, every substance has one fundamental property that is essential to it. Substances which are bodies have the property of *extension*. 'Extension' is a term philosophers use to refer to the way things take up space, or their physicality (imagine a point 'extending' itself in space to become a line, then a two-dimensional figure, then a three-dimensional figure). Although the particular extent of a body is subject to change, the property of *extension as such* is not removable or changeable. Descartes also believed there were non-physical substances, minds, which have the essential property of *thinking*. Just as extension is essential to what it is to be a body, thinking is essential to what it is to be a mind. These essential properties, extension and thinking, Descartes called 'principal attributes', whereas he called changeable properties 'modes' of those attributes. Substances, for Descartes, are either 'extended substances' (bodies) or 'thinking substances' (minds), and these two kinds of substance are fundamentally different. Descartes posited, and attempted to demonstrate, a necessarily existing infinite thinking substance, God, who creates and sustains the existence of all these substances.

A seventeenth-century Cartesian, then, believed that the world is made up of an enormous number of substances, some of them minds and others bodies, whose existence is made possible by a necessarily existing God. Figure 1.1 represents this common-sense view of multiple substances with their principal attributes.

Spinoza's objective in Part I is to convince readers that their common-sense, Aristotelian–Cartesian view of a world of multiple, individual substances is wrong. He does this by letting readers discover that if they start with *good definitions* of terms like substance, attribute and God, they will *not* arrive at the conception of reality described by Descartes or Aristotle. They will, instead, work through Spinoza's propositions and arguments to arrive at the *true* conception of reality: a single substance equivalent to God.

Definitions

This is why Spinoza begins Part I with *definitions*. If we are going to make use of terms like substance and attribute in order to understand

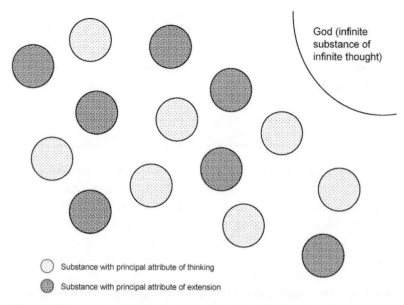

Figure 1.1 The seventeenth-century common-sense view of the world

reality truly, we need to start with a clear understanding of those terms.

When you look at the definitions of Part I, you might ask yourself: Are the definitions *true*? This very question was put to Spinoza in a letter from his readers (Letter 8, CW 778–80). Spinoza's answer is: It depends on what you mean by truth. Definitions may be accurate descriptions of real things, as in the definition of a mammal. In this case, the definition is true in the sense that it coincides with what is real. Alternatively, definitions may be clear explications of how we understand certain terms, as when we define a radius from the nature of a circle. The truth of this definition does not consist in its coinciding with really existing circles and radii. The definition of a radius is true because it is fully explained from the nature of a circle, whether or not any circles actually exist. Similarly, an architect's 'definition' of a temple is true if it is fully and properly understood from basic physical principles, whether or not it is ever actually built (Letter 9, CW 791–2).

This is the kind of truth that Spinoza's definitions have. A good definition is one that is well-conceived; it is understood clearly, distinctly, fully and consistently. A bad definition is one that is poorly conceived, unclear, partial or inconsistent. Good definitions, like the definition of the radius, include the grounds by which they are justified and require no appeal to real things. So, what matters is not whether the terms defined relate to reality, but how well their ideas are conceived. Spinoza does believe his definitions are true, and moreover, he believes that they correspond perfectly to reality. But it is not the correspondence of the definitions to reality that makes them true. Rather, what makes the definitions real is the intrinsic truth of the ideas behind them. That intrinsic truth will not be fully understood by us until we have finished reading the *Ethics*. For now, Spinoza asks us to accept them on trust – for the purpose of argument – knowing that as we follow his argument, their intrinsic truth and reality will become apparent to us.

Spinoza defines ideas that his readers believe they already understand. In so doing, he clarifies our understanding of these ideas, revealing that our concepts of substance, attribute, mode and God are not as clear and consistent as we imagine.

Let us now look at some of the definitions in detail. Things are likely to seem a bit patchy and incoherent until everything comes together around Proposition 15. Be patient, read carefully and things will soon fall into place.

D1 states: 'By **cause of itself** I understand that whose essence involves existence, or that whose nature cannot be conceived except as existing.' If you think about this, you will see what Spinoza means. Something which *causes itself* brings about its own existence; logically, it must already exist in order to bring about its own existence. It exists 'prior' to its own existence. A being that is cause of itself, then, cannot *not exist*. Its nature cannot be conceived as not existing. In other words, it is in its very nature to exist; its essence involves existence.

The existence of 'cause of itself' must be of an eternally active nature. For if this thing had to exist 'prior' to its own existence, it cannot be the case that it ever 'started' to cause its own existence (to start to cause its existence would require that it already existed, which would require that it already caused its existence, and so on). Nor could it 'finish' causing its existence and continue to exist. This thing must be eternal, not only in the sense of eternally existing, but in the sense of eternally bringing about its existence. The essence of 'cause of itself' is to exist as the eternal activity of 'actualising' itself. It exists both as the power to cause its actuality and as the actual effect of its own causal power.

Now read D3: 'By **substance** I understand what is in itself and is conceived through itself.' To understand this definition, we need to understand what Spinoza means by the word 'in'. When Spinoza uses phrases such as 'in itself' and 'in another' (as in D5), 'in' does not mean 'inside'. Rather, 'in' denotes a relation of logical dependence. What is 'in itself' depends logically on itself. What is 'in another' depends logically on another thing: that other thing is *prior in nature* to it.

Substance *is in itself*; this means that a substance depends, for its being, on itself alone. Similarly, the concept of a substance is not formed from the concept of another thing. A substance is not understood through the concept of something else, but rather *is conceived through itself* alone. A substance requires nothing beyond itself to exist and a true understanding of it requires nothing outside of the concept of the substance itself. In other words, a substance is that which is ontologically and epistemologically independent and self-subsistent. Note that Spinoza's definition of a substance does not contradict the seventeenth-century common-sense view, which similarly understands a substance to be independent. Spinoza does not disagree with that view; he merely clarifies it.

Skip ahead to D5: 'By **mode** I understand the affections of a substance, or that which is in another through which it is also conceived.' Whereas a substance *is in itself*, a mode *is in another*. The being of a mode depends on the being of another thing which is logically prior to it, and the mode can be truly understood only through the concept of that logically prior other thing. This means that in order for a mode to *be*, and in order for it to *be conceived*, something else must already be and be conceived. The mode is defined as 'the affections of a substance', which means the changeable properties of a substance. So the being that is logically prior to the mode is a substance, and a mode is dependent on substance, both in its being and in its being-conceived. In Part I, Spinoza uses the words 'mode' and 'affections' interchangeably. The mode is a mode of substance or its affections: the changeable properties that are ontologically and epistemologically dependent on a substance.

From D1, D3 and D5, we understand what a substance is, in its most basic definition. A substance is, simply, *that which is* prior to, and independent of, its modes. At its most basic, a substance is pure, indeterminate being. This pure, indeterminate being *is* and *is conceived*. The very first principles of reality are that *there is being* and *there is conceiving of being*. A substance depends on itself alone for its being, strongly suggesting that it is 'cause of itself', the eternal activity of causing its existence. If that suggestion turns out to be right, then *being as such* is the power of making itself actual.

We now need to look at Spinoza's definition of **attribute** in D4. This is a difficult concept to grasp. The definition of attribute as 'what the intellect perceives of a substance, as constituting its essence' can be misleading. Spinoza does not mean that each person's intellect perceives a substance in a different way. Nor does he mean that attributes are subjective illusions or 'mere appearances'. But he does mean that attributes are the different ways in which a substance *can be* perceived. The intellect can truly perceive a substance, but not as pure, indeterminate being. The intellect always perceives a substance *as* one of its attributes. An attribute *is the substance itself*, as perceived in a certain way.

To clarify this, adopt the position of the seventeenth-century common-sense reader. You believe that the world is full of substances, as defined in D3, and that those substances can be perceived by the intellect. But what we perceive is not *substance as such*. That is, in our sensory experience and thinking we never perceive pure, bare 'being'. Rather, we perceive being *as* one of two kinds: either physical bodies or minds. We perceive substances *as* extended things and *as* thinking things. Descartes understands extension and thinking to be fundamental properties of substances. But Spinoza disagrees. For him, extension and thinking are not properties of a substance, but rather two different 'ways' that a substance can be perceived. Extension and thinking are two *expressions* of the essence of substance (as Spinoza puts it at P10S). Attributes are the ways in which the essence of a substance is expressed and perceived. It is incoherent to think of a substance without an attribute, because the intellect necessarily perceives substance *as* one or more of its attributes.

Spinoza will demonstrate later in the text that extension and thinking are two of the attributes of substance. At that point it will also become clear why Descartes, along with the common-sense reader, is wrong to think of attributes as properties. Attributes are not properties of a substance and they are not separable from a substance. Attributes constitute *what the substance exists as.*

These four definitions are what we need most for what is coming next. We will not examine the other four in detail now, but do read them over. This is all bound to be somewhat perplexing at first, but if you have some sense of what Spinoza means by cause of itself, substance, attributes and modes, you now have the basic building blocks of Spinoza's ontology.

Axioms

The seven axioms that follow the definitions are Spinoza's basic logical principles. He takes them to be self-evident, eternal truths. For example, 'whatever is, is either in itself or in another' (A1): anything that has being is either an ontologically independent substance or an ontologically dependent mode. Spinoza thinks that this, and all the other axioms, are basic, uncontroversial statements of logical relation.

Some of the axioms may not appear to you to be self-evident. Take A3 and A4, which look particularly strange. A3 says that effects follow necessarily, and only, from causes that have the specific qualities, or *determinations*, required to produce those effects. In other words, every effect has a determinate cause, which is logically prior to that effect. This means, first, that every effect has a cause, and second, that every effect is 'in' its cause: the existence of the effect depends logically on the existence of the cause. Similarly, the knowledge of the effect depends on the knowledge of its cause (A4). For example, water is the cause of rain. Rain depends on water, both in terms of its being and in terms of the true understanding of it: there is no being of rain without the prior being of water, and you cannot fully know what rain is without knowing what water is. The being and knowledge of the effect (rain) depend on the being and the knowledge of the cause (water).

An important implication of A3 is that, given a specific determinate cause, its effect will *necessarily* follow. When water exists in a way that includes all the determinations necessary for rain, rain will follow necessarily. An important implication of A4 is that knowing something truly means understanding how it follows from its cause. If we are to understand rain truly, we must truly understand how it follows from the nature of water. Spinoza believes that effects are 'in' their causes and are unfolded from them. This metaphysical way of thinking about causation seems alien to us now, but in the seventeenth century it was far more prevalent than the empirical model of cause and effect that we are familiar with today. That is why Spinoza states A3 and A4 as axioms, which he would expect all his readers to accept.

We are now ready to look at Spinoza's propositions. Each proposition, along with its demonstration, is an argument for a specific point, with the propositions building and combining to form argumentative arcs. (The whole book can be seen as one big arc, encompassing numerous smaller arcs.) We shall look in detail at the arc that stretches from P1 to P14, in which Spinoza seeks to convince us that there is only one substance, and that is God.

Propositions 1–5
Remind yourself of the seventeenth-century common-sense view by looking at Figure 1.1. In this first stage of the argument, Spinoza seeks to demonstrate that there cannot be two or more substances of the same attribute. That is, there cannot be multiple substances sharing the attribute 'thinking' or multiple substances sharing the attribute 'extension'. Let us see how Spinoza gets there and why this is significant.

P1 states that a substance is prior to its affections (i.e. its modes). This is evident from the definitions, as Spinoza says, since the modes depend on substance for their being, whereas substance depends only on itself. Substance must be logically and ontologically prior to its modes.

P2 tells us that two substances having different attributes have nothing in common with one another: they are two separate beings that are perceived in two separate ways. Each substance exists independently and is conceived independently, so the being of one does not 'involve' the being of the other, and the concept of one does not 'involve' the concept of the other. They are ontologically and epistemologically distinct. Since their being is not 'involved' (i.e. one is not bound up in the other) and their concepts are not involved (the concept of one is not bound up in the concept of the other), these two substances cannot be causally related in the sense described in A3 and A4 (P3).

In P4 we learn that there are two ways of distinguishing substances from one another: either they are distinguished by existing as different attributes or they are distinguished by having different affections (modes). This is because reality consists of nothing but substances (as their attributes) and the modes of substances, so there is no other way to distinguish them.

Up to now, Spinoza's definitions and propositions have not broken with the Cartesian position. The seventeenth-century common-sense reader can accept Spinoza's definitions and axioms, and P1–4, without challenging his own world-view. With P5, however, things change, for this is where Spinoza makes his first major break from the common-sense view. He argues that in nature there cannot be two or more substances of the same attribute. This is significant because if Spinoza is right, there cannot be multiple thinking substances (human minds) or multiple extended substances (bodies), as Descartes believed. Because it is so important, we shall look at P5 in some detail.

Spinoza's question in P5 is this: *can there be more than one substance of the same attribute?* Descartes thought that there could be multiple substances of the same attribute, as we can see in Figure 1.1. To test Descartes' position, let us examine three substances, depicted in Figure 1.2. Substances A and B share the same attribute, but differ in their modes (represented by the differently shaped 'surface manifestations' of the substances). Substances B and C have different attributes, and also differ in their modes.

Now, look at the demonstration for P5. If there were two or more distinct substances, they would have to be distinguished from one another either by a difference in their attributes or by a difference in their modes; that was demonstrated in P4. Let's take each of these options in turn.

First, assume that two substances are distinguished from one another by a difference in their attributes, as substances B and C are in Figure 1.2. In this case, the two substances have different attributes and can be distinguished. But if different attributes are the *only* way to distinguish substances from one another, then two substances with

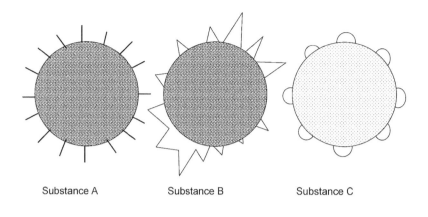

Substance A   Substance B   Substance C

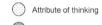   Attribute of thinking

Attribute of extension

Figure 1.2 Distinguishing substances in IP5

the *same* attribute (A and B) cannot be distinguished. They are both pure, indeterminate being, perceived as extension. There is no other way of distinguishing A from B, so they must be the same substance. Therefore, there is only one substance of the same attribute.

Next, consider whether A and B could be distinguished from one another by the difference in their modes. In this case, Spinoza says, we are merely talking about a difference of mode, and not about a difference of substance. The fact that the modes are different does not mean that the substances are distinct. This is because substance is prior to its modes (P1), and substance is understood through itself, not through its modes (D3). In order to compare the substances *as such*, we must 'put the modes to one side' and consider the substances in themselves. When we ignore the surface manifestations and consider the substances in themselves, substances A and B cannot be distinguished from one another, so they must be the same substance. Therefore, there is only one substance of the same attribute.

This is more easily understood if we remember that attributes are *what the substance exists as*. Two substances sharing the same attribute exist as, and are perceived as, the same thing. The attributes cannot be taken away to reveal two different substances underneath, for a substance without its attributes is just pure, indeterminate being. An attribute is the most basic determination of being. Two substances with the same basic determination cannot be distinguished; therefore they are the same thing. There cannot be multiple substances sharing the same attribute.

Problems with P5

A problem with Spinoza's demonstration has probably already occurred to you. Spinoza argues that two substances having the same attribute are, in fact, *only one substance*. But couldn't there be two substances with the same attribute that are numerically distinct, i.e. standing side by side in space, as A and B are in the figure?

The answer is no, for the simple reason that substances are not *in space*. For Spinoza, space is not a container for substances, but a mode of substance. If space were a container for substances, its existence would be independent of substances. That would mean space was itself a substance that other substances were dependent on, which would contradict D3. Spinoza understands space to be among the modes that we must 'put to one side' in P5. Substances are *prior* to space and thus cannot be considered as having positions *in* space. For this reason, there could not be two 'duplicate' substances with the same attribute sitting side by side. If you can imagine two substances as having the same attribute, you are really thinking of one substance.

Here is another problem that might have occurred to you. Doesn't Spinoza jump illegitimately from the conclusion 'two substances with the same attribute cannot *be distinguished* from one another' to the claim that 'two substances with the same attribute cannot *be distinct*'?

For Spinoza, these two statements are the same. It is not merely the case that we human beings cannot distinguish one substance from another. It is logically impossible to do so. There simply are no grounds for the distinctness of substances other than their having distinct attributes. If two substances share an attribute, they are not distinct.

If we accept P5 – and Spinoza thinks we *must* accept it – then our world-view necessarily changes. No longer do we believe in the world of Figure 1.1. Our world now looks more like Figure 1.3.

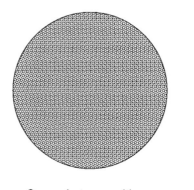 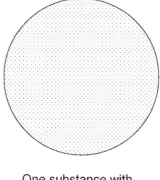

One substance with
attribute of extension

(One extended being)

One substance with
attribute of thinking

(One thinking being)

Figure 1.3 Our view of the world after IP5

Propositions 6–10

With P5, Spinoza has shown that there cannot be multiple substances sharing the attribute 'thinking' or multiple substances sharing the attribute 'extension'. Since there cannot be two or more substances of the same attribute, there can be only one thinking substance and one extended substance. That leaves open the possibility that there are multiple substances, since there can be as many substances as there are different attributes. The purpose of the next set of propositions, 6–14, is to show that there is only *one* substance with *all* the attributes, and that is God.

Let us continue to imagine that there are at least two substances, as in Figure 1.3. P6 tells us that since these substances have nothing in common – their different attributes mean they have different essences, after all – they cannot cause or produce one another. Since (according to P5) every substance has a different attribute, no substance can be the cause of another substance. A substance must therefore be 'cause of itself'. We already suspected this from reading D1 and D3, but Spinoza demonstrates it at P7. As cause of itself, it is in the nature of a substance to exist. Therefore, 'it pertains to the nature of a substance to exist' (P7); the essence of a substance involves existence. This means that substance is both cause and effect of itself.

Substance is the power of bringing about its own being; it is the activity of making itself actual.

Spinoza goes on to argue that every substance is necessarily infinite (P8). For a thing to be finite, it must be limited by something else of the same nature (D2): a plant is prevented from growing infinitely large, or living infinitely long, by other physical things that limit it. But a substance cannot be limited by something else of the same nature, because there are no two substances of the same nature (P5). Therefore, a substance cannot be finite; it must be infinite in its existence. Furthermore, Spinoza says, it follows from P7 that substance is infinite. It pertains to the nature of substance to exist: its essence includes existence. But being finite involves a negation of existence – at some point the finite thing will cease to exist. But the essence of substance involves existence; it cannot involve the negation of existence. Substance is infinite being or infinite self-actualisation: it is 'an absolute affirmation of existence' (P8S1).

Spinoza pauses here to acknowledge the difficulty of what he has just demonstrated. The demonstrations of P7 and P8 themselves are not difficult, but the ideas that Spinoza has unfolded are. We now see, perhaps for the first time, that ordinary finite things in the world cannot be substances. And we see that substances do not have a beginning and end in time, or limitation in space, as everyday things do. Scholium 2 to Proposition 8 breaks out of the grid of demonstrations and gives us time to reflect, in everyday prose, on the strangeness of what has been demonstrated.

Spinoza reminds us that the truth of P7 is already bound up in the nature of substance. If you accept that there is some being that is ontologically independent, then you must accept that that being is cause of itself and exists necessarily. And if you accept that, then you must also accept that ordinary things in the world are not ontologically independent substances, but finite *modes* of substance. Starting with a good (ie. clear and consistent) definition of substance as that which is in itself and is conceived through itself – a definition that no Cartesian would disagree with – Spinoza has shown us that it is logically inconsistent to believe that everyday things are substances. We must abandon the Cartesian common-sense view altogether.

Up to now, we have been considering substances that have one attribute each. But in P9 and P10, Spinoza reveals that a substance can have more than one attribute, and indeed, the more 'reality or being' a thing has, the more attributes belong to it. In other words, if a substance has *more being*, there is more of what it is. There may be two, three or more ways of perceiving what it is. This means a substance could have two, three or more attributes that express what it is. Indeed, a substance could have infinite attributes, infinite ways in which its reality, or being, is expressed. And, according to D6, a substance of infinite attributes would be God.

P11: The Necessary Existence of God

This brings us to Spinoza's proof for the existence of God in P11. 'God, or a substance consisting of infinite attributes, each of which expresses eternal and infinite essence, necessarily exists.' Spinoza's demonstration is very short: if you think you can conceive of God not existing, then, by A7, his essence does not involve existence. But P7 demonstrates that it pertains to the nature of substance to exist, because substance is cause of itself. It would be absurd to say that the essence of a substance of infinite attributes did not involve existence. Since God is that substance (by D6), God exists necessarily.

You may initially find this demonstration unsatisfying. It may appear to you that Spinoza's argument is a variant of an 'ontological proof for the existence of God' like those of Descartes and Anselm, in which God's existence is 'demonstrated' from the fact that the *concept* of God includes the *concept* of necessary existence. Those arguments are unconvincing because they do not recognise that necessary existence in the concept does not imply necessary existence in actuality.

But Spinoza's proof for the existence of God is not an argument of that kind. Spinoza does not argue from the concept of God to his existence; he argues that a substance of infinite attributes cannot *not exist*. God is defined as a substance consisting of infinite attributes, each of which expresses infinite essence (D6). That means God is pure being, perceived *as every attribute* there is. Each of those infinite number of attributes expresses an infinite amount of essence. So God comprises every way that being expresses itself, and every way that being can be perceived, to an infinite extent. Every substance exists necessarily (P7), but God exists necessarily in a special way: it exists necessarily as *every way* that being can be expressed. Spinoza thinks you cannot truly conceive this substance not to exist, because this substance is *being as such*. For if *being as such* did not exist, there would be no being and no conceiving of anything at all.

Here is another way to understand Spinoza's proof. Think carefully about what has already been demonstrated about substance. A substance is not a 'thing', but the *power* of actualising its own existence. A substance of one attribute actualises itself infinitely (P8), but only *as* one type of being: as extended things, for example. A single-attribute substance is therefore non-actual with respect to all the other attributes. But a substance of *infinite* attributes has an infinite amount of reality, being and power. It actualises itself as infinite types of being with respect to *every* attribute. There is no attribute which this substance does not actualise itself as. A substance of infinite attributes is an infinite power that makes itself actual in every way possible. If this substance were non-actual, it would not be that power to actualise; it would not be substance at all. Thus, a substance of infinite attributes is *necessarily actual*. Its essence involves existence, not only logically but *actually*.

Recognising the difficulty of P11, Spinoza gives us three 'alternative' demonstrations. But these alternatives are really no easier to understand than his original demonstration, because they all rely on and return to the original demonstration. The first alternative argues from the impossibility of a cause that would limit or take away the existence of God. Because of the nature of God as a substance of infinite attributes, that cause can neither be within God's nature nor outside it, so no such cause is possible and God must necessarily exist. The second alternative argues from the existence and power of finite beings. If a substance of infinite attributes can not exist, then finite beings which do exist have more existence and power than that substance. But the non-existence of that substance – being as such – would mean the non-existence of those finite beings. Since we ourselves and other finite beings do exist, it must be that a substance of infinite attributes exists too. The third alternative, in the Scholium, is a version of the 'actualisation' argument explained above.

In short, Spinoza argues that you cannot conceive the non-existence of God because you cannot conceive the non-existence of *being*. God, or a substance of infinite attributes, is *being as such*, which is expressed in infinite ways to an infinite extent. That is why 'there is nothing of whose existence we can be more certain than we are of the existence of an absolutely infinite, or perfect, Being – that is, God' (P11S). God is 'complete' in that its being comprises all the being that there is. This is what Spinoza means by the term 'perfection' introduced towards the end of P11S.

Problems with P11

Many readers, even if they accept the cogency of Spinoza's arguments in P11, still resist his conclusion that God necessarily exists. You may be in that position now. If so, ask yourself: Why do I find P11 difficult to accept? Here are some suggestions and responses.

1. *You accept that Spinoza has demonstrated the existence of a substance consisting of infinite attributes, but not the existence of God.* It's true that what Spinoza demonstrates in P11 is the existence of 'a substance consisting of infinite attributes'. He defines God as this substance in D6. Spinoza's definition of God is not arbitrary; he believes that all philosophers and religious authorities would agree that the essential nature of a divine being is to be a substance with infinite attributes expressing eternal and infinite essence. That is, the definition of a divine being includes ontological independence, infinite power and eternal being. If you accept that P11 demonstrates the existence of a substance of infinite attributes, and if you accept that the being that has these qualities is what we understand by 'God', then you must accept that P11 has demonstrated the existence of God.

2. *You follow Spinoza's argument, but do not believe in God and so you cannot accept Spinoza's conclusion.* See the response to 1, above. If you do not believe in God, what you do not believe in is probably the God of the Bible. Spinoza does not demonstrate the existence of *that* God; he demonstrates the existence of a substance of infinite attributes. He thinks we ought to call this substance 'God' because what we truly understand by 'God' is a substance of infinite attributes. But just as we are not compelled to give the name 'square' to a four-sided figure, we are not compelled to give the name 'God' to a substance of infinite attributes. If you prefer, you can call it being, substance, power or nature. You cannot not believe in *being*; so you cannot not believe in Spinoza's God.

3. *You follow Spinoza's argument, but you believe in a personal God and so cannot accept Spinoza's definition of God.* See the response to 1 and 2,

above. Spinoza says that the God you believe in is *essentially* (if you abstract from all its other qualities) a substance of infinite attributes. The God of the Bible, or of any religion, is truly understood to be a substance of infinite attributes, but is mistakenly *represented* by human beings to be an anthropomorphic figure who intervenes in human affairs. Spinoza wants to convince you that you should truly understand God as infinite substance, rather than believing in the 'image' of God as portrayed by organised religion.

4. *You accept that Spinoza has demonstrated the necessary existence of God in a logical sense, but still cannot accept that God actually exists.* Re-read the explanation of P11, above. If you're still not convinced, look at a study such as Mason (1997).

5. *You believe that Spinoza's argument is invalid or his premises are not acceptable.* Work through the definitions and propositions prior to P11 to determine where you think the problem is. If you cannot find a problem but are still convinced there is one, look at a critical analysis such as Bennett (1984), and decide whether you think the objections to Spinoza are good ones.

This is one of several points in the text where Spinoza causes us, even today, to challenge our own ideas about reality. Spinoza knows we are likely to resist his claims, but he also believes that his claims are true and that, if we think them through clearly, we cannot *truly* reject them. Of course, the reader is not obliged to accept Spinoza's argument for the existence of God, and if his argument is weak, then we should not accept it. But if his argument is plausible, then we should put our presuppositions to one side and work with Spinoza's conclusion. As an experiment, try living with the belief that God is *being as such* and that all being is God. As we read more about Spinoza's God, we must actively work to understand God as being and not to imagine the anthropomorphic God of the Bible.

Propositions 12–14

The next important proposition, bringing us to the end of this argumentative arc, is P14. After two propositions (P12 and 13) in which he demonstrates that a substance cannot be divided, Spinoza says that 'except God, no substance can be or be conceived'. In other words, God, or *being as such*, is the only substance there is. If you have read the explanation of P11 carefully, you will see immediately why this is. God is a substance of infinite attributes, each one of which expresses infinite essence. If there were a substance other than God, it would have to have at least one attribute. But this attribute would have to be one of the infinite attributes pertaining to God's essence. By P5, no two substances of the same attribute can exist. So it follows that except God, no substance can be or be conceived.

In other words, each attribute pertains to only one substance (P5). God has *all* the attributes; so God is the one and only substance. God is infinite being expressed in every way possible. There is no other 'being' that another substance could 'be'.

Spinoza has now demonstrated that reality consists of one substance, God, and that God is infinite being with infinite essence. *God is being itself,* and for this reason it is logically impossible to think of God as not existing. If you can imagine God as nonexistent, you are not thinking of God consistently; it is not possible to disbelieve in being or to be sceptical about being. *Being is,* and it is expressed in infinite ways. God is thinking being, God is extended being and God is being as every other attribute too. This is expressed in the two corollaries to P14. In nature there is only one, absolutely infinite substance (P14C1). Therefore, thinking things and extended things – everyday minds and bodies – are not substances or independent beings (P14C2).

P14C1 suggests that God is 'in Nature'. But since God is absolutely infinite substance, God cannot be within nature or dependent on it. What Spinoza means here is that throughout all of Nature there is only one substance, and it is God. In other words, God *is* Nature. This is expressed by a famous phrase Spinoza uses later in the book: 'that eternal and infinite being we call God, or Nature' (IV Pref.). The word 'or' here denotes the identification of the terms 'God' and 'Nature'. God, substance, Nature: these are interchangeable terms referring to one infinite being that expresses itself in infinite ways.

Our picture of reality now looks very different. It is an inversion of the Cartesian picture of Figure 1.1. We now understand reality to be *one* substance, God, which exists as infinite attributes. Figure 1.4 represents Spinoza's reality after P14, but be careful not to let it mislead you. God/substance/Nature is *infinite* and *active,* two qualities which cannot be adequately depicted in the figure.

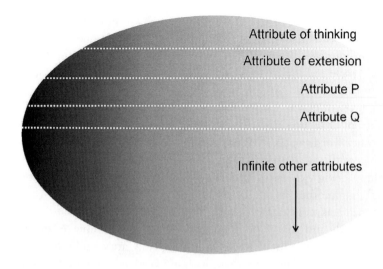

Attribute of thinking

Attribute of extension

Attribute P

Attribute Q

Infinite other attributes

Substance, God, or Being

Figure 1.4 Our view of the world after IP14

God's Causality and Freedom

The view that all reality is *one being* is called monism, and you can see now why Spinoza is considered a monist. One implication of monism is that all entities, including ourselves and the things around us, are somehow parts of one single being. Furthermore, since there cannot be any 'gaps' or divisions in substance (P13), we must be *continuous* parts of that being. But if Spinoza is right that all being is one, why does our experience seem to reveal a world of differentiated, individual beings? What causes us to feel that we are emphatically distinct from the things and people around us? If we are 'parts' of substance, i.e. parts of God, does that mean God is like a patchwork made up of all the things in existence?

While answers to some of these questions will have to wait until Part II, the latter question is answered in the next few propositions. Human beings and all the individual entities of our world are indeed parts of God. But we are not 'parts of God' in the way that books are parts of a library or in the way that cells are parts of your body. A library would not exist without its books and your body would not exist without its cells. But God *does* exist prior to all the finite things in the world and is the cause of their existence. In other words, finite things are not *constitutive* of God. Rather, God's infinite being causes and expresses itself as an infinite number of things.

This is what Spinoza means when he says 'whatever is, is in God' (P15). Remember that for something to be 'in' God means that it depends ontologically on God. Whatever is – all that exists – depends on God for its being, and nothing can exist without God. Similarly, nothing can be conceived without God. Everyday finite things are *modes* of God. All things in the universe, including ourselves, are the affections, or finite changeable properties, of God or Nature.

Because God's nature is infinite, the number of modes that follow from God's nature is also infinite. Furthermore, these infinite modes follow from God's nature *with necessity*: 'from the necessity of the divine nature there must follow infinitely many things in infinitely many modes' (P16). When Spinoza refers to 'the necessity of God's nature', he means what follows necessarily from God's essence. From the essence of any thing, a number of properties necessarily follow; the essence of snow is to be white and cold, for instance. But God's essence is infinite and has an infinite amount of being. Infinite properties, or modes, will therefore follow from it, not randomly but *necessarily*. Just as 'coldness' follows necessarily from 'snow', *everything in existence* follows necessarily from God. This is made clearer if we remember that God is not a thing, but is the activity of actualising its being. God is a power of actualising its essence, of actively 'unfolding' the modes that follow necessarily from its essence. God therefore causes all things as 'cause of itself'.

An important implication of this is that 'God alone is a free cause' (P17C2). Turning back to D7, we see that what is free 'exists from the necessity of its nature alone, and is determined to act by itself alone'. Indeed, this definition accords well with one version of our common-sense understanding of freedom, namely the idea of autonomy or self-determination. God is cause of itself and cannot be determined to act by any other substance (since there is no other substance), so God is *free* in the sense that God causes and determines itself. But God is not free in the sense of having free 'choice' about what it causes (see P32C1). God is not a 'person' who chooses what to actualise. God is the power of actualising what necessarily follows from its essence. God is free because God acts from the necessity of its own nature.

It is important that we do not imagine that God is somehow constrained by the necessity of its own nature. If you do imagine that, it is because you are thinking of God as a monarchical figure who has certain possibilities and constraints. It is all too easy to lapse into this assumption, as Spinoza is well aware; the long Scholium to P17 is intended to make us think carefully about this point. God has neither possibilities nor constraints. God's essence is infinite being that actualises itself necessarily and infinitely. Perhaps you imagine that 'acting from the necessity of its nature' means that there are certain things that God is incapable of actualising. This is correct in a certain sense: God is incapable of actualising anything that falls outside its nature, i.e. anything that logically cannot have being. But it is not the case that there is a storehouse of 'possible' beings that, due to God's nature, God is prevented from actualising. *All possible being* is necessarily actualised, because God's essence *is* the actualisation of all possible being.

Spinoza stresses, therefore, that to deny God free choice is not to deny God any power, because the very idea of 'God's free choice' is contradictory. Think about it: if God had the freedom to choose what he created, then God could bring it about that what is in his own essence was not actualised. But that is to say that God could destroy or nullify part of his own nature, and that would contradict the essence of God as self-actualising *being as such*. Some philosophers believe that there is an infinite number of 'possible' beings that God conceives but does not actualise. But, Spinoza says, this position *denies* God power, because it implies (a) that 'God understands infinitely many creatable things which nevertheless he will never be able to create', and (b) that had God created all those things, God's power would be exhausted (P17S). Spinoza banishes *possibility* and affirms that infinite being is necessarily actualised, thereby affirming God's infinite power. Spinoza's God does not conceive things and then choose to create or not create them; God *is* the things it causes. There is and can be *nothing else*.

This brings us to P18: 'God is the immanent, not the transitive, cause of all things.' What does Spinoza mean by this? It is evident that God must be the *cause* of all things. This follows from the fact that all things are in God and are conceived through God (see the three corollaries to P16). Descartes would not have disagreed that God is the cause of all things; indeed, he attempts to prove this himself. But Descartes means that God is a *creator*, separate from the things he creates. To say that God is a creator is to say that God acts on some other substance external to himself.

Spinoza's God is evidently not a creator in this sense. For Spinoza, it is impossible for God to *act on* something that is *other* than God, or to create something *separate* from God, because there is nothing other than God. God is therefore not a 'transitive cause'. God's causality of modes is the actualisation of its own being; the modes that are caused by God remain 'in' God. That is what it means to be an 'immanent cause'. God's causality is immanent in that the effects of God's causality remain 'in' God and are part of God. God's causality of the modes is not like an artist's creation of sculptures. A better analogy is the way in which you cause your facial expressions. Modes are the ways the essence of God expresses itself (see P25C).

The idea of immanent causality is wrapped up in the notion of God as 'cause of itself'. As we noted earlier, that which causes itself is both the *cause* of itself and the *effect* of itself. The effects of God's causality remain *in God*. As cause of itself, God is the power of self-actualisation – substance. As effect of itself, God is that which is actualised – the modes. That is why Spinoza says 'God must be called the cause of all things in the same sense in which he is called the cause of himself' (P25S). This distinction within God between that which causes and that which is caused, between the power to actualise and the actualised effects of that power, is expressed at P29S as the difference between *Natura naturans* and *Natura naturata*. *Natura naturans*, or 'nature naturing', refers to God as cause of itself, as substance which acts freely. *Natura naturata*, or 'nature natured', refers to God as effect of itself, as the modes that are caused and determined.

There is debate in the secondary literature about whether Spinoza believes we are properties that inhere in God or effects that are caused by God (see Nadler 2007: 81–3). The answer is that we are both. As modes we are properties of substance, and as effects we are caused by substance. There is no incompatibility here, because God causes its properties immanently, much as you cause your facial expressions. The language of properties is not very helpful when considering how particular things are in God (Spinoza seldom uses the term). Particular things are modes by which God's attributes are expressed in a certain and determinate way (P25C). That is, we are the finite and changeable expressions of God as extension, and God as thinking.

Spinoza's Universe

Now we need to understand how Spinoza believes God's causality works to produce a universe. This is one of the most obscure topics in the *Ethics*: Spinoza says very little about it, and what he does say is open to a number of different interpretations. This interpretative openness should, I think, be seen as a strength. First, Spinoza's lack of precision about the organisation of reality is a reflection of the limitations of human knowledge. For reasons that will later become clear, there is only a certain amount that a finite mind *can* know about God, and Spinoza sticks to what he knows with certainty. Second, Spinoza's very general account of the workings of God's causality enables readers of any historical era to understand the universe truly, regardless of scientific advances.

What does Spinoza actually tell us about the structure of the universe? The relevant propositions are P21–5, which have some of the most difficult demonstrations in the book. Spinoza tells us this: what immediately follows from the absolute nature of any of God's attributes, is a thing that is infinite and eternal (P21). Because this thing is the effect of God's causality 'as' one attribute, this thing is a mode, and scholars have come to call it an 'immediate infinite mode'. Spinoza tells us, next, that what follows from the *modified* nature of any of God's attributes – i.e. whatever is caused by the immediate infinite mode, in the same attribute – must itself be infinite (P22). This we shall call the 'mediate infinite mode'. P23 tells us that every infinite mode is caused in one of these two ways. P24 and 25 tell us that the essences of these infinite modes do not involve existence and are caused by God. Finally, the Corollary to P25 says that particular things are modes by which God's attributes are expressed 'in a certain and determinate way'.

If you find this material impossible to visualise or understand, you'll be relieved to hear that Spinoza's contemporary readers did not find it any easier. Georg Hermann Schuller, writing on behalf of Ehrenfried Walther von Tschirnhaus, both members of a reading group that discussed a draft of the *Ethics*, wrote to Spinoza for clarification of this material. 'I would like examples of those things which are produced immediately by God, and those which are produced by the mediation of some infinite modification,' Schuller writes (Letter 63, CW 917). Spinoza replies directly:

> The examples you ask for of the first kind are: in the case of thought, absolutely infinite intellect; in the case of extension, motion and rest. An example of the second kind is the face of the whole universe, which, although varying in infinite ways, yet remains always the same. (Letter 64, CW 919)

It is not certain what Spinoza means by 'absolutely infinite intellect' or 'motion and rest', let alone 'the face of the whole universe', but with this material we can develop a plausible interpretation of P21–5. God, or substance, has infinite attributes. Of these infinite attributes, we can conceive of two: thinking and extension. God exists as thinking being, and God exists as extended being. So thinking being and extended being *as such* exist necessarily and eternally. (Note that Spinoza has not yet demonstrated that thinking and extension are two of God's attributes, which explains why he does not speak of any specific attributes at P21–5. He will demonstrate these specific attributes in Part II, but we need to assume them here in order to understand what follows.)

Because each of the attributes has infinite essence, what follows from the nature of the attributes must also be infinite. This means that each of the attributes expresses an *immediate infinite mode*: there is an infinite way in which thinking is expressed and an infinite way in which extension is expressed. What follows from the nature of 'thinking being' as such is the infinite intellect, i.e. infinite true understanding. What follows from the nature of 'extended being' as such is infinite motion and rest. Infinite intellect and infinite motion and rest are caused *immediately* by the *absolute nature* of God's attributes. In other words, infinite thinking being necessarily includes, causes and expresses itself as infinite intellect. Infinite extended being necessarily includes, causes and expresses itself as infinite motion and rest.

Now, from each of these *immediate* infinite modes follows a *mediate* infinite mode. The mediate infinite mode is what Spinoza calls 'the face of the whole universe' in Letter 64. These faces 'vary in infinite ways, yet remain always the same'. To clarify what is meant by 'face of the whole universe', Letter 64 directs us to a later passage from the *Ethics*, IIL7S. IIL7 is one of a series of propositions in which Spinoza tells us that each individual is composed of many other individuals, forming a series increasing in complexity. For instance, multiple cells and micro-organisms make up a fish; multiple fishes, plants, stones and water make up a river; multiple rivers, mountains and land make up the earth; multiple planets make up the universe, and so on.

And if we proceed in this way to infinity, we shall easily conceive that the whole of nature is one individual, whose parts, that is, all bodies, vary in infinite ways, without any change of the whole individual. (IIL7S)

This is what Spinoza means by 'face of the whole universe'.[1] It is the whole of nature as one infinite individual, which is composed of an infinite number of individuals, each of which encompasses a series of individuals. (We shall discuss this theory further in Part II.) Now, this infinite individual is expressed both in the attribute of thinking and in the attribute of extension, so it has two 'faces'. Insofar as this infinite individual is caused by infinite motion and rest, it is *an infinite physical individual*. Insofar as it is caused by infinite intellect, it is *an infinite thinking individual*. That is, all the physicality in the universe exists as part of one physical individual and all the thinking in the universe exists as part of one thinking individual. For this reason, we can think of the infinite mediate modes as *a single, infinite continuum of physicality* and *a single, infinite continuum of thinking*.

Finally, the finite modes are the 'surface features' of these infinite continua. Finite modes of extension – physical things – are the temporary, changeable expressions of the infinite continuum of physicality. Finite modes of thinking – minds and ideas – are the temporary, changeable expressions of the infinite continuum of thinking. Finite

---

[1]   Translators disagree about the term 'face'. Spinoza's Latin term is *facies*, which, if linked to the verb *facio* (to fashion or make), could be translated as 'the fashioning' or 'the make' of the whole universe (Hallett 1957: 34). While the term 'make' reminds us that the mediate infinite mode is (like all of substance) active, the term 'face' evokes a surface continuum that *expresses* finite modes (see Figure 1.5).

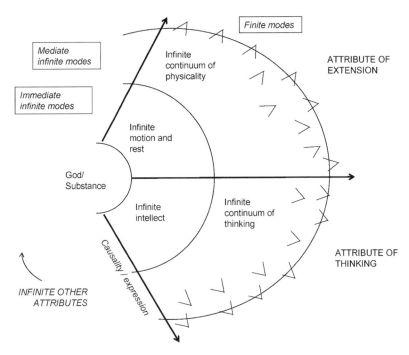

Figure 1.5 Spinoza's universe

modes are determined to be what they are by the infinite modes that constitute their 'depth'.

Figure 1.5 visualises this material to make it clearer. It represents God/substance as a sphere that is constantly active in actualising itself. The figure shows two 'segments' of that sphere, i.e. two of an infinite number of attributes. God exists as extended being and as thinking being (among infinite other ways of being). As extended being and thinking being, God causes (or *expresses*) the immediate infinite modes: infinite motion and rest, and infinite intellect. They, in turn, cause (or express) the mediate infinite modes: the infinite continuum of physicality and the infinite continuum of thinking. The finite modes, represented by the spikes, are the 'surface features' which rise and fall from those continua. Imagine the continua as the surface of the ocean; finite modes are the waves on the ocean, which come into existence, last a certain amount of time and then fall back into the infinite continuum from which they came. The waves are determined to be what they are by the 'depth' of the ocean that causes them.

Figure 1.5, and the analogy of the ocean, are aids to understanding Spinoza's universe. But remember that no figure can adequately capture the activity or infinitude of God. Do not let Figure 1.5 mislead you into thinking that God is a closed and static sphere. Nor should you be misled into imagining that God is *separate* from its modes or that any of the modes are truly separate from one another. God is the whole infinite sphere, all of which is one being and is not limited to the semi-circle on the left.

Spinoza's Universe and the Sciences

Questions remain about Spinoza's universe. What exactly *is* the infinite continuum of thinking? Or infinite motion and rest, for that matter? How are we supposed to make any sense, in the real world, of Spinoza's complex metaphysical story about substance causing its modes? To answer these questions, let us consider another way of interpreting this material: as a model for explaining the scientific derivation of things. Curley (1988) advocates a version of this scientific reading; it seems to me not implausible that Spinoza upheld some version of it too. Spinoza sees metaphysics and science as two practices that aim to understand reality truly; metaphysical and scientific interpretations are two different, and complementary, ways that the same activity of substance can be understood.

Look at Figure 1.5 and consider it in the following way. God, as extended being, causes there to be motion and rest. In other words, extended being expresses itself as an infinite dynamism that contains within it all possible dynamic relations. 'Infinite motion and rest' is the infinite set of variations of motion, which expresses all possible ways that physical beings can exist. This 'all possible ways' can be understood as a single continuum of *laws of motion*. This encompasses not only the laws about how bodies move, but the entire body of laws – chemical, microbiological, quantum-mechanical – of how physical bodies are constituted. The nature of each finite physical being is explained through, and determined by, these laws. Physical bodies are modes of a single continuum, or body, of physical laws, which follows from infinite motion and rest, which follows from God's nature as extended being.

This means that there exists a body of true and eternal physical laws that determines how finite bodies are caused. Those laws are not human inventions or abstractions; they are part of God and truly determine physical bodies. Through scientific experiment and rational thinking, human beings have achieved some true knowledge of some of these eternal laws, and we are capable of achieving more. In 'Part II : Minds, Bodies, Experience and Knowledge', we shall see why this is. For now, note that Spinoza's system leaves room for an infinite number of future scientific discoveries, since there is an infinite amount of true physical law.

We can consider the attribute of thinking in a similar way. God, as thinking being, causes there to be infinite intellect: true understanding of everything that exists. Infinite intellect expresses itself as a single continuum of thinking. This continuum is made up of infinite relations of true understanding: the laws of logic. Just as physical laws determine and explain the nature and relations of bodies, logical laws determine and explain the nature of minds and relations of ideas. Human minds are modes of true understanding, and our thinking follows from this logical order. When we have true knowledge, we understand according to the order of logical principles in the infinite intellect. This is one reason why the *Ethics* is composed using the geometrical method. True knowledge is understood logically, and the *Ethics* is a textual representation of true knowledge. The geometrical method best approximates how true ideas are *truly* connected in God.

Determinism

We understand now what it means to say that 'God must be called the cause of all things in the same sense in which he is called the cause of himself' (P25S). God's self-actualising activity is the activity through which the modes are caused and through which they continue to be (P24C). Finite modes are caused through infinite ones, as Figure 1.5 shows. What, then, does Spinoza mean when he says that every finite mode is determined to exist and produce effects by another finite mode (P28)? How is it that the existence of finite modes is caused *both* by God *and* by other finite modes?

Finite things are determined to be the kinds of things they are through the causality of the infinite modes. A puffin is determined to be able to fly at its characteristic rate by virtue of the dynamic relations, in infinite motion and rest, from which its nature follows. The essence of the puffin is explained through those relations. But the existence of that particular puffin is not part of its essence (P24) and is not explained through relations of motion and rest. Nor can the specific encounters and events in the life of the puffin be explained through physical laws. Its beginning to exist is explained through its having been produced by two parent puffins, whose existence is explained through production by their parents, and so on. The puffin's continuing to exist is explained by its getting enough fish to eat, which is explained by the fish getting enough plankton to eat, and so on. And its encounters are explained through the interactions of an infinite number of causal factors that make up the world it lives in. In fact, to *explain fully* the existence of any particular thing, we have to appeal to an infinite nexus of causes – the entire continuum of physical being.

On Spinoza's account, God causes the puffin in two ways. God causes the essence of the puffin to be what it is, insofar as God exists as infinite intellect and infinite motion and rest. But God causes the existence of that individual puffin insofar as God exists as the parent puffins (and their parents, and their parents' parents, and so on). For this reason, the determination of the finite modes through the infinite modes (P25C) is compatible with their being determined to exist and produce effects by another finite mode (P28). The complete causal story of the puffin's existence is therefore in God, insofar as God constitutes both the metaphysical 'depth' of the universe and the surface 'breadth' of the universe. To fully understand any individual finite mode, we must understand God.

The existence of every finite thing is caused by another finite thing (P28). So God is not a creator who forms individual things and beams them into existence. Nor did God create the world, or the universe, in this way. All finite modes, including the earth, the sun and the stars, are caused by God *as* other finite modes.

From this we can see the emergence of Spinoza's determinism. God's self-actualisation occurs according to the necessity of God's nature, meaning that finite modes exist and cause one another according to that necessity (P29). Just as the actualisation of God's being is not contingent, the order in which things happen is not contingent – that is, it could not have happened in a different way from how it does happen. When Spinoza says there is nothing contingent in nature (P29), this means that there is nothing which 'might or might not' have happened. There are no alternative universes or 'possible worlds' that God could have created but didn't. In Spinoza's universe, all being is necessary and actual; nothing is merely 'possible'. It is only from the perspective of our own ignorance about the future that we say that things are contingent or that they 'might or might not' happen (P33S). From God's perspective, all things that can happen do happen and are necessarily determined to happen. They can be produced in no other way or order, because God could not be other than it is (P33).

From God's supreme power, or infinite nature, infinitely many things in infinitely many modes, that is, all things, have necessarily flowed, or always follow, by the same necessity and in the same way as from the nature of a triangle it follows, from eternity and to eternity, that its three angles are equal to two right angles. (P17S)

Spinoza's universe is, then, fully determined. One implication of this is that human beings are fully determined in their thoughts and actions; that is, we have no free will. This can be inferred from P32, which argues that the will is not a free cause, but a necessary one. If there is an infinite will (like the infinite intellect), then it is a mode of God. All modes are determined, so an infinite will could not be free (in the sense defined in D7). *God itself* is free, as cause of itself. But God's will and intellect, as effects of that causality, are not free. Human will and intellect, which are finite modes of God, are therefore not free either. We human beings are finite modes, and all our being and actions are effects of the infinite, necessary unfolding of God. We shall return to Spinoza's denial of free will in 'Part II: Minds, Bodies, Experience and Knowledge'.

God or substance is the ongoing activity of self-actualisation. Its causality is the infinite unfolding of its own essence, and its effects are its own infinite and finite modes that unfold from it according to the necessity of its nature. God's power is to actualise its essence according to the necessity with which it unfolds. In other words, 'God's power is his essence itself' (P34). This proposition nicely sums up Part I, in which we have struggled to understand how being is God and how God is active causal power.

The Appendix: Spinoza's Genealogy of Prejudice

After the difficulty of Part I, the Appendix comes as something of a relief. The Appendix to Part I is Spinoza's engaging and provocative critique of commonly held 'prejudices'. These include the Biblical image of an anthropomorphic God, the notion of intelligent design and the moral concepts of good and evil. Spinoza seeks to diagnose the natural and historical reasons why people hold these prejudices, an exercise that anticipates Nietzsche's 'genealogy' of moral values in *On the Genealogy of Morality*.

Spinoza believes that all these prejudices depend on the doctrine of final causes. A 'final cause' is the aim or purpose for the sake of which a thing exists or acts. Human beings believe that their own actions are directed towards purposes, and thus tend to believe that other natural beings, all of nature and God itself are similarly purpose-oriented. This doctrine of final causes leads to a number of related beliefs, such as:

- the belief that God acts with an intention or purpose;
- the belief that God has organised the world for the sake of human or divine purposes;
- the belief that natural things exist for the sake of human or divine purposes;
- the belief that the universe has a final purpose, and that the universe is moving towards fulfilling that purpose.

These beliefs characterise the Christian world-view as it was in the seventeenth century. This was the doctrine set by the Church and held to be incontrovertible. Philosophers were expected to fit their metaphysical ideas to this doctrine, because it was taken to be the unquestionable basis of all further investigation. Spinoza, of course, cannot accept this doctrine, since it contradicts what he has demonstrated to be the case about God and the universe. He argues that these beliefs are *superstitions* that do not reflect the truth.

The doctrine of final causes derives from basic human experience, Spinoza says, and has historically become entrenched as religious doctrine. In earliest times, human beings were ignorant of the true causes of things but conscious of being driven by their desire to seek their own advantage. Naturally enough, humans believed that they acted intentionally, according to their purposes in fulfilling their desires. Being ignorant of any other cause, they assumed that their intentions provided the sole explanation for their actions, which led them to believe that they acted from freedom of will. They were therefore satisfied with explaining events according to final causes and with appealing to their own purposes in particular: it seemed to humans that all events must be freely willed and intentionally organised to suit their own ends. This fallacy was supported by their experience of nature, which seemed to provide numerous means for fulfilling their desires: 'eyes for seeing, teeth for chewing, plants and animals for food, the sun for light, the sea for supporting fish . . ..' Hence, they consider all natural things as means to their own advantage' (I App.). Not having created these things themselves, human beings naturally assumed that they had been created for them by a 'ruler of Nature' endowed with intentions and free will.

From there developed the image of a God who intentionally designs and directs nature for the good of humankind, who expects worship in return and who rewards the pious and punishes the impious. The fact that 'conveniences and inconveniences happen indiscriminately to the pious and the impious alike' did not make them reassess their image of God, but led them to give up explaining God's purposes and to conclude that God's ways are inscrutable to man. Were it not for mathematics, Spinoza says, humanity would have been trapped in this ignorance about God forever. Mathematics helps us out of this predicament because it is not concerned with final causes, but with the essences and properties of figures: it shows us 'another standard of truth', one that does not depend upon experience.

To put it simply, human beings developed an image of God based on a maximised version of their own abilities and tendencies. That is because *every* finite mode naturally regards things from its own perspective. As Spinoza puts it, humans think of God as eminently human; if a triangle could speak, it would say that God is 'eminently triangular' (Letter 56, CW 904). Our human-centric view of the world leads us to judge things and events according to what is most useful to us. Consequently, human beings have developed a series of value-terms with which we judge natural phenomena: good, evil, order, confusion, beauty, ugliness, etc. Since people have different experiences and different purposes, we disagree with one another and differ in our judgements. It is only from some particular human perspective that nature has 'order', that a flower is 'beautiful' and that a hurricane is 'evil'. From the perspective of God, none of these terms is relevant; God is nature, and nature *is*. God has no purposes and makes no judgements.

True knowledge does not reflect the perspective of human beings, triangles or any other finite modes. As we have seen, the true idea of God is not of a king-like figure who acts according to freely chosen and mysterious purposes, creates order and beauty, and is pleased by human goodness. When truly understood, God is a substance of infinite attributes (D6), the infinite self-actualisation of being. Spinoza's God does not make choices and does not act for the sake of purposes; it does not design individual beings or a harmonious universe; it does not judge or intervene in events. Spinoza's God is being itself, with no purpose set before it. 'For if God acts for the sake of an end, he necessarily wants something which he lacks' (I App.).

Importantly, Spinoza's God is *not mysterious*. Much of God's nature and power may be unknown to us, but *God is being* and is fundamentally knowable. Whenever we gain true knowledge about the world, we gain more true knowledge of God. Knowledge of God is to be gained through mathematics, science and philosophy, not through religious texts or the doctrine of priests. If this were not enough of a challenge to Church authority, the strong implication of the Appendix is that any organised religion that promotes an anthropomorphic image of God, or any of the other prejudices discussed here, is guilty of obfuscating the truth. Theological doctrine is superstition that keeps people ignorant. Only by breaking free of this superstition will we be able to seek true understanding of the universe, thereby gaining true insight into God.

You can see why Spinoza was unable to publish the *Ethics* in his lifetime. His rejection of the fundamental beliefs promoted by the Church is explicit and absolute. His demand that we understand God as *being* leads us to understand God as something that exists physically as well as intellectually, that can be scientifically examined and understood, that exists as all things and that is indifferent to human goodness and suffering. He requires us to recognise no difference between God and nature, and to understand all things as part of God. It should now be perfectly clear why Spinoza was branded an atheist and his work banned for over a hundred years after it was written.

Part II: Minds, Bodies, Experience and Knowledge

Part II of the *Ethics* is called 'On the Nature and Origin of the Mind'. Spinoza's focus is on the *nature* of the mind and its *origin* – that is, its causal origin in God/substance. Part II is primarily about how a finite mind is related to God. Only once we understand that basic relation can we begin to truly understand the nature of the body, the nature of experience and the knowledge available to us.

Part II, then, contains Spinoza's epistemology, or theory of knowledge. But Part II is also about bodies and contains Spinoza's theories of physics, individuality, sensation, experience and memory. It is in this section that the empiricist elements of Spinoza's thought become as prominent as the rationalist ones. Here he demonstrates his *parallelism*, probably the most counterintuitive idea we are confronted with in the *Ethics*. Indeed, Part II is more difficult than Part I in terms of the number of topics Spinoza presents and the ideas he asks you to accept. In this part Spinoza will try to convince you that thoughts do not cause actions, that most of your knowledge is imaginary, that inanimate objects have minds and that you have no inner 'self'. But despite its complexity, Part II is more engaging than Part I in that Spinoza is talking about recognisable minds and bodies, such as your own mind and body and those of the objects around you. The aim of this section is to enable you to find your way through the complex ideas of Part II by looking at the topics that Spinoza treats, in the order in which they arise in the text.

What is an Idea?

As in Part I, Spinoza starts Part II with definitions and axioms. Right now we shall focus on just two: D1, where Spinoza defines 'body' as a mode that expresses God's essence insofar as he is considered as an extended thing, and D3, where Spinoza defines 'idea':

By idea I understand a concept of the mind which the mind forms because it is a thinking thing.
Exp: *I say concept rather than perception, because the word perception seems to indicate that the mind is acted on by the object. But concept seems to express an action of the mind.* (D3)

Now, turn back to Figure 1.5. Our model of Spinoza's universe includes the finite modes as the 'surface features' of God/substance.

These finite modes are the expression of God's being *as* extended being, or *as* thinking being. D1 confirms that those modes that express God's essence *as* extended being are physical bodies. This conforms to the scientific interpretation of Spinoza's universe too: physical bodies are determined through God's ongoing activity as the laws of motion and rest.

Finite minds, then, are the expression of God as thinking being. However, while D1 refers to finite bodies, D3 does not refer to finite minds. Whereas a body is 'a mode that . . . expresses God's essence insofar as he is considered as an extended thing' (D1), Spinoza says that the mind forms an idea 'because *it is* a thinking thing' (D3, emphasis added). This tells us that D3 refers not to human minds, but to 'God's mind', i.e. God as a thinking thing. God alone *is* a thinking thing (all other minds are *modes* of thinking), so 'the mind' referred to in D3 is God/substance, considered as a thinking thing.

Remember, when we say that 'God is a thinking thing', we do not mean that God is a static thing that happens to think. Rather, in accordance with our understanding of God as infinite self-actualising activity, we mean that, among the infinite ways that *God is*, God is the *activity of thinking*.

D3 tells us that ideas are concepts formed by God's activity. This does not mean that God 'creates' ideas separate from itself (remember IP18). Ideas are immanently caused by God's activity and remain part of God. But what is an idea? Look at Spinoza's explanation of the definition. An idea is not the result of the action of something else on the mind (perception); it is the activity of thought itself (conception). An idea is 'an action of the mind'. It is the activity of God as thinking thing. But God as thinking thing *is* the activity of thinking. That means there is no real difference between *God's mind* and *God's idea*: both terms refer to God as the activity of thinking as such.

God's idea actualises itself *as* infinite and finite modes of thinking. Finite thinking modes, therefore, express God's idea in a certain and determinate way: they are finite ideas, or finite minds. As we shall see, every mind is an idea; a finite mind is nothing other than a determinate mode of thinking activity. Finite minds/ideas are expressions of God's essence as thinking, just as finite bodies are expressions of God's essence as extension.

So it is important that we do not think of an idea as a picture or representation. Nor should an idea be understood as a proposition or a fact. Furthermore, we must not confuse Spinoza's sense of 'idea' with other philosophers' uses of that term. Spinoza's 'ideas' are not the same as Descartes', Locke's, Hume's or Kant's 'ideas'. For Spinoza, an idea is an activity of thinking; the *idea of* something is the active conceiving of that thing; and to *have an idea* is to partake of God's thinking activity.

The Attributes of Thinking and Extension

Since the beginning of 'Part I: Being, Substance, God, Nature' we have been working under the presupposition that thinking and extension are two of God's infinite attributes. Here, Spinoza demonstrates that we were justified in making that presupposition, because 'thought is an attribute of God' (P1) and 'extension is an attribute of God' (P2). We know this to be true simply from the certainty that we think (A2) and the certainty that we feel our body to be affected in many ways (A4). Our thoughts and bodily sensations, since they are modes of substance, must be conceived through some attribute of God. Since thoughts can be logically conceived only through thinking, and since bodily sensations can be logically conceived only through extension, thought and extension must be attributes of God.

Here arise some questions. First, note that Spinoza takes it to be indisputable that 'man thinks' and that 'we feel that our body is affected in many ways' (A2 and A4). Spinoza does not take seriously Descartes' doubt about the existence of the body or his scepticism about the nature of bodily sensation. Why is Spinoza so sure that *sensation* is conclusive evidence for the existence of physical bodies and therefore the attribute of extension? Isn't it possible that sensations and physical bodies are illusions generated by the mind and that what appears to be extended being is really produced through the attribute of thinking? If that were the case, P2 would be incorrect and thinking would be the only demonstrable attribute of God. The converse challenge can also be put to Spinoza. Why is he so sure that our thoughts must be explained through the attribute of thinking? Couldn't it be the case – as some materialist philosophers believe – that thinking is explained purely through the physical structures and chemicals of the brain? If that were true, P1 would be wrong, and extension would be the only demonstrable attribute of God.

Let us consider how Spinoza responds to the challenge that physical sensations might really be thoughts. Spinoza does not, at this point, demonstrate or assume that physical bodies exist. He merely states that *we feel a certain body, i.e. our own body, to be affected in many ways.* That we feel bodily sensations cannot be denied; what is in question is the cause through which those sensations exist and are conceived. That cause must be God, and it must be God *as* some attribute. Could it be God as the attribute of thought? Clearly our *thoughts about* these sensations involve the attribute of thought. But Spinoza is suggesting that the sensations themselves involve something that cannot be caused through pure thinking and cannot be truly understood by reference to thinking alone. If there were a creature that *only thought* and had no physical being, not only would that creature be unable to *feel* sensation, it would also be unable to *understand* sensation. Sensation is therefore caused and conceived through something other than pure thought: the attribute of extension.

Spinoza's response to the second challenge – that thinking might really be a physical process – is even more basic. The cause of our thinking could not be God as the attribute of extension, because the activity of thinking must be *conceived through* the activity of thinking. To say that thinking is *conceived* through *extension alone* would be absurd, since 'conceiving' necessarily involves thinking. So for *anything* to be conceived, thinking must be an attribute of God.

To the insistent materialist, however, Spinoza has not justified the claim that thinking and conceiving *could not* be understood as a purely physical expression of God's essence. Ultimately, Spinoza's response seems to be that thinking *just is* fundamentally different from extension, in which case there is a hidden assumption that thinking and extension are different in kind. You may be tempted to accuse Spinoza of maintaining a dualism that is unjustified and inconsistent with his monism.

I believe Spinoza would respond by saying that being does indeed involve a basic duality (that does not amount to dualism) for which further justification cannot be demanded. There is a fundamental difference between *thinking* and other expressions of being, which goes right to the heart of Spinoza's ontology. Substance *is*, and substance *is conceived* (ID3); a duality between being and thought is part of the very nature of God/substance. Thinking is different from God's infinite other attributes, in that all those other attributes must be *conceived through* thinking. This duality does not disturb Spinoza's monism, since God/ substance is one being regardless of how its attributes are expressed. The duality consists in the fact that one of God's infinite attributes – the attribute of thinking – is distinct from all the others, and it alone has an epistemic relation to all the others. The true nature of the attribute of thinking, then, is what justifies Spinoza's 'hidden assumption'.

Parallelism

The idea that all the attributes must be *conceived through* the attribute of thinking is expressed in P3. Because thinking is one of God's attributes there is necessarily 'in God' an idea of its own essence and of every-thing that necessarily follows from it. That is, ideas of each of God's attributes, and ideas of every mode in every attribute, follow necessarily from God as thinking activity. These are comprehended by the infinite intellect (see P4Dem). Infinite intellect contains and expresses the ideas *of* extension, thinking and the infinite other attributes; and the ideas of every mode of extension, every mode of thinking, and every mode of the infinite other attributes. So for every attribute, and for every mode in every attribute, there exists an idea in the infinite intellect.

P5 is written in unfamiliar language, but the proposition is not difficult to grasp. Ideas are caused not by the things that they are ideas of, but rather by God as a thinking thing. For example, the idea of a boat is not caused by the existence or perception of a physical boat, but by God as thinking being. Look back to Figure 1.5 and you will see exactly why this is. All ideas are caused by God *as* the attribute of thought and are comprehended in the infinite intellect. From the infinite intellect there follows an infinite thinking continuum; finite ideas are the 'surface features', or expressions, of that continuum. Finite ideas are thus the 'end point' of a process of causation that has occurred through the attribute of thinking alone. Ideas, however and wherever they occur, are not caused by extended objects. God causes ideas *only insofar as it is a thinking thing*, not insofar as it is (also) an extended thing.

The same argument applies to extension and to all the other attributes too. Physical bodies are caused by God through the attribute of extension alone. God, as extended being, causes infinite motion and rest. Infinite motion and rest 'comprehend' all physicality (just as infinite intellect comprehends all ideas). From infinite motion and rest there follows an infinite physical continuum, with finite bodies the surface features, or expressions, of this continuum. Bodies are caused only through the attribute of extension, just as ideas are caused only through the attribute of thinking. As Spinoza says,

The modes of each attribute have God for their cause only insofar as he is considered under the attribute of which they are modes, and not insofar as he is considered under any other attribute. (P6)

You can see 'parallelism' emerging here, since Spinoza argues that there are parallel streams of causality operating in each of the attributes. God/substance exists as an infinite number of causal streams which do not interact with one another. Some implications of this are already evident. Ideas do not cause bodies and bodies do not cause ideas. That means that God's ideas of things are not the basis of their production; nor do human ideas cause physical effects. Ideas are not caused by physical bodies themselves. Perhaps most startlingly, there would seem to be no causal interaction between our minds and our bodies. If that is right, how does Spinoza explain the correspondence between what we think and what we feel and do?

The answer is Spinoza's theory of parallelism, and P7 is where its thesis is stated: 'the order and connection of ideas is the same as the order and connection of things'. Now, we already know that bodies and ideas have entirely separate streams of causality (P6). And we already know that God has an idea of every mode of extension (P3). Spinoza is now claiming that bodies and ideas have *parallel* streams of causality; that the order of causality is *the same* in the attribute of thinking as it is in the attribute of extension. This is a truly remarkable claim, but has an incredibly short demonstration. Spinoza simply refers us to IA4. We need to unpack this further.

IA4 states that knowledge of an effect depends on knowledge of a cause. (The word 'knowledge' is interchangeable with 'idea' for present purposes, since both refer to the activity of conceiving something truly.) You now understand this in a way that you didn't when you read it the first time. With your new understanding of parallel streams of causality, you can see that Spinoza is saying that effects follow from causes (IA3), and that in a parallel stream, *ideas* of those effects follow from *ideas* of those causes (IA4). Imagine a simple causal chain, such as this one:

Egg → larva → caterpillar → chrysalis → butterfly

In each case the effect *follows from*, or *is caused by*, its cause; this cause is caused by a previous cause, and so on to infinity. These effects are physical bodies and they are caused solely through the attribute of extension. Now, according to IIP3, God has the idea of each one of these physical bodies. These ideas do not interact with the bodies, because they exist in a separate causal stream in the attribute of thinking. But that separate causal stream unfolds in the same order as the physical one, because *knowledge* (i.e. an idea) of the effect follows from, or is caused by, the idea of the cause, and this idea is caused by an idea of the previous cause, and so on:

Idea of egg → idea of larva → idea of caterpillar →
idea of chrysalis → idea of butterfly

If this seems difficult to understand, look back at the explanation of IA4 in 'Part I: Being, Substance, God, Nature'. You can't know what a chrysalis is unless you first know what a caterpillar is; and you can't fully understand a caterpillar unless you first understand a larva. Just as the effect *exists through* the cause, the idea of the effect *is conceived through* the idea of the cause. And the order of physical things is exactly the same as the order of ideas, because the things correspond exactly to their ideas.[2] Figure 2.1 shows how the streams of causality are parallel between bodies in the attribute of extension and their ideas in the attribute of thinking.

The egg and the idea of the egg; the larva and the idea of the larva; two parallel streams of causality, unfolding in the same order and connection. In one stream, physical things exist; in another stream,

---

[2] It might be objected that this is an example of change in one individual, and not an example of causality *between* individuals. But for Spinoza, the difference is only one of perspective. A caterpillar becoming a butterfly can also be understood as one individual causing the existence of another (see IVP39S). Similarly, one billiard ball causing motion in another can be understood as change in a single individual (i.e. the whole billiards-game; see IIL7S). And of course, all causality amongst finite modes can be understood as mere variations of the whole of nature. In any case, Spinoza's parallelism is equally valid for intra-body change and inter-body causality.

ATTRIBUTE OF EXTENSION

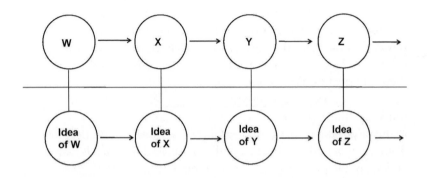

ATTRIBUTE OF THINKING

Figure 2.1 Parallelism

their ideas are known. But these two streams (i.e. the attributes of extension and thinking) are simply two ways in which the causality of God/substance unfolds. Since the causality of God/substance unfolds necessarily, extension and thinking are *two ways* in which that *single activity* of causal unfolding can be perceived. A thing and its idea are therefore the *same mode* expressed through different attributes.

The thinking substance and the extended substance are one and the same substance, which is now comprehended under this attribute, now under that. So also a mode of extension and the idea of that mode are one and the same thing, but expressed in two ways. (P7S)

Each thing is expressed both as a mode of the attribute of extension and as a mode of the attribute of thought. So every physical thing is also an idea and every idea is also a physical thing. This is represented in Figure 2.1. W and the Idea of W are not two things; they are *one thing* expressed through two attributes. Thinking and extension are two ways in which the same mode exists.

Now consider this: God's essence unfolds necessarily, in the same order, in *every attribute*. P7 is therefore valid not only for thinking and extension, but for the infinite other attributes as well. This means that each mode exists across every attribute. In other words, the *same finite mode* is expressed as physical thing, as idea, as a mode of attribute P, as a mode of attribute Q, etc. If Figure 2.1 could be infinitely expanded to show all the attributes, it would show that each of the modes W, X, Y and Z were connected to modal expressions in each of those other attributes as well. As Spinoza puts it, 'things as they are in themselves' (i.e. considered from the absolute perspective of God) exist, and are caused, through *all* the attributes (P7S). From God's perspective, each finite mode is, and is conceived, in infinite ways.

From a limited human perspective, however, finite modes are evidently *not* conceived in infinite ways. We are not conscious of our own existence in these mysterious other attributes. Human beings perceive only bodies and thoughts (A5), and therefore conceive things only through the attributes of extension and thinking. Why is the human mind limited to perceiving just these two attributes? We must read further to find out.

Human and other Minds

Since human beings are finite modes, they exist like the modes represented in Figure 2.1. Each human is *one mode*, existing *both* through the attribute of extension *and* through the attribute of thinking (and through all the other infinite attributes as well). The body and mind are therefore *one thing*, expressed in different ways. Spinoza demonstrates this in P11–13.

First, he shows that the human mind is constituted by the idea of a singular thing which actually exists (P11). Remember that ideas are the *active conceiving* of things, formed by God and comprehended in God's infinite intellect (D3, P3). Recall also that a mind is nothing other than an idea, i.e. a mode of thinking. A finite mind is the idea of an existing finite thing, so your mind is *God's active conceiving* of some finite thing. 'From this it follows that the human mind is a part of the infinite intellect of God' (P11C). Our minds are finite expressions of the infinite continuum of thinking, which is the expression of infinite intellect. Our minds are 'in' the infinite intellect, that is, part of God's true understanding.

Specifically, each mind is God's true understanding of one particular finite thing. Whatever happens in the existing finite thing is comprehended in its corresponding idea – that is, everything that happens in the thing is perceived by the mind (P12). Now, each mind does perceive things happening to, and following from, a body – exclusively one body, its own body. So the 'idea' that is our mind corresponds to an object that is our body (P13). The mind is the idea of the body; the body is the object of the mind. What you think of as 'your' mind is really God's idea of a certain extended finite mode ('your' body).

It follows that 'man consists of a mind and a body, and that the human body exists, as we are aware of it' (P13C). You may be reminded here of Descartes' assertion that the human being is a mind connected to a body. But Descartes is a dualist who believes that mind and body are different types of substance. Spinoza obviously does not accept that, and importantly, he rejects Descartes' claim for the independence of the mind from the body. For Spinoza, the mind is the *idea of* the body and is therefore identical with it. The mind must not be understood as an independent substance or spirit connected to, or dwelling within, the body. The mind is not a separate thing connected to the body. For Spinoza, mind and body are *one individual* expressed through the attributes of thinking and extension. Consider mind and body as two ways in which a thing is seen, through two different lenses of a microscope. 'The mind and the body are one and the same individual, which is conceived now under the attribute of thought, now under the attribute of extension' (P21S).

Spinoza therefore deftly avoids Descartes' problem of mind–body interaction. Descartes was unable to offer a convincing explanation of how mind and body interact, given that they are supposed to be different kinds of substance with nothing in common. For Spinoza, this problem does not arise. First, mind and body are not substances at all; second, causal interaction between the attributes of thinking and extension is ruled out (P6). There can therefore be no interaction between mind (a mode in the attribute of thinking) and body (a mode in the attribute of extension). But mind and body perfectly correspond to one another, because the mind is the idea of the body and, due to parallelism, everything that happens in the body happens also in the mind. The mind comprehends everything that happens to the body, but does not cause any effects in the body. And the body's experiences do not cause ideas in the mind, but these experiences are directly and truly *known* by the mind. If mind and body are one thing, seen under different lenses of the microscope, then it is incoherent to talk about interaction. Similarly, there can be no question of the reduction of mind to body, or body to mind. Since mental events and physical events are the same events, seen under different lenses, it is incoherent to suggest that mental events could be reduced to physical events, or vice versa. On the contrary, every physical event in the body is also a mental event, as it is actively comprehended in the mind.

Here is a problem that may have occurred to you. Since the mind is the idea of the body, the mind must include ideas of *everything* that happens in the body. That is the content of P12: 'if the object of the idea constituting a human mind is a body, nothing can happen in that body which is not perceived by the mind.' If Spinoza is right, then our minds must have true knowledge of everything that goes on in our bodies. Yet our experience suggests this is not the case. We don't have direct mental awareness of what goes on in our inner organs, for instance, and we don't truly understand how our DNA replicates itself. Indeed, the vast majority of our bodily activity goes undetected by our minds. How does Spinoza's claim that *the mind is the idea of the body* square with the very limited knowledge we seem to have of our bodies?

Spinoza thinks we cannot understand these limitations of our knowledge until we understand more about the *human* mind and the *human* body. For what he has shown so far, Spinoza says, is 'completely general' and does not pertain exclusively to human beings. In other words, *all* extended beings have minds. *Every* mode in the attribute of extension (and indeed every other attribute) has a corresponding *idea*, and that is what is meant by 'mind'.

The things we have shown so far are completely general and do not pertain more to man than to other individuals, all of which, though in different degrees, are nevertheless animate. For of each thing there is necessarily an idea in God, of which God is the cause in the same way as he is of the idea of the human body. And so, whatever we have said of the idea of the human body must also be said of the idea of any thing. (P13S)

Minds, then, are not the exclusive preserve of human beings. Cats, caterpillars and bacteria have minds; stones, trees and rivers have minds; pencils, factories and sewing machines have minds. Since all these things are modes of God, God necessarily has the idea of each of them in the infinite intellect. The minds of cats, stones and sewing machines are therefore part of the infinite intellect, and those minds, like our own, comprehend everything that happens in their bodies.

It would, of course, be absurd to suggest that cats and caterpillars have minds to the same extent that human beings do, let alone stones and sewing machines. The difference is one of complexity. Finite modes differ greatly in their 'excellence' or 'reality'. This is not a value judgement: Spinoza means that some modes have more qualitative features than others and are able to *do* more. Since an idea corresponds perfectly to its object, a body that is more active and able corresponds to a mind that is more active and able. As the human body is far more complex and capable than the body of the stone, the human mind is far more complex and capable than the mind of the stone. But the stone certainly thinks to *some* extent, the cat to a greater extent and the human being to a greater extent still. And just as nature contains individuals with bodies that are more capable than those of human beings, nature contains individuals whose thinking is more complex than that of human beings. Like the stone, the human being's thinking will be limited in line with the capabilities of its body.

To understand the capabilities of the human mind, then, we need to understand something of the human body. This explains why P13 is followed by a short section on the nature of bodies: to explain 'the difference between the human mind and the others, and how it surpasses them . . . and also to see the cause why we have only a completely confused knowledge of our body' (P13S).

Bodies, Individuals and Capabilities

Set out through axioms and scientific *lemmata*, the section between P13 and P14 contains Spinoza's theory of bodies. This includes his theory of individuality, his description of the mechanics of sensation and his sketch of some basic physical laws. These are the laws that follow from the nature of motion and rest as such, and are part of the infinite body of physical laws that *cause and determine* physical finite modes. (You may find it helpful here to re-read the sub-sections of 'Part I: Being, Substance, God, Nature' on 'Spinoza's universe' and 'Spinoza's universe and the sciences'.)

As we saw in 'Part I: Being, Substance, God, Nature', the *mediate infinite mode* of the attribute of extension is understood both as the infinite body of physical laws and as an infinite continuum of physicality. Spinoza describes this as 'the face of the whole universe': all of physical reality is a single physical continuum which contains and expresses every finite body. In 'Part I: Being, Substance, God, Nature', I used the analogy of the ocean to make this clearer. The infinite continuum of physicality is like the surface of the ocean, which varies as waves form, move, rise and fall. The waves are not separate from the ocean; they exist and move in it, and eventually disappear by collapsing back into it. The finite modes are like waves, 'surface features' of an infinite continuum of physicality, existing and moving within that continuum.

This suggests that physical bodies – your body, the chair you are sitting on, the floor beneath you, the air around you, the person next to you – are really one continuous physical body. Since everything is 'in' God/substance (IP15), and since substance cannot be divided (IP13), there can be no 'spaces' between things. But if all physical reality is one single continuum, how are physical bodies distinguished from one another?

We already know that individual bodies are not substances, and so they cannot be said to be distinct on the basis that they are ontologically independent of one another. Instead, Spinoza says in L1, bodies are distinguished from one another by their different rates of motion and rest. Your body is distinct from the chair because it has a certain rate of motion that differs from that of the chair. Neither your body's nor the chair's rate of motion is fixed: to be sure, bodies move at different speeds at different times and are caused to move by other bodies that affect them (L2, L3). But individuals differ in their capacities for motion and rest, and in the ways they are able to move and be moved. Although you and the chair may both now be at rest, only *you* will move if the fire alarm sounds. That is what makes you and the chair distinct individuals. Nothing physically distinguishes one individual from another except this difference in capacities for motion and rest.

But there are circumstances in which a person and a chair can be understood as one individual. For example, when a human body communicates its motion to a wheelchair and the wheelchair reciprocally communicates its motion to the human body, then both move together at the same rate. In this case, the person and chair are one individual (see the Definition after A2′). You may find this a strange way to think about individuality, because it does not recognise the integrity of the human as a *person* distinct from objects. For Spinoza, individuality is based on *relations of motion*, not personhood, and for this reason individuals exist on a number of levels. Certainly, the human body in this example is an individual in its own right and so is the wheelchair. But when the human and the wheelchair communicate their motion to one another in 'a certain fixed manner', they form a bigger, composite individual that *moves as one*. Similarly, a group of person-wheelchair individuals moving together (in a race, for instance) form a still bigger, multi-composite individual.

A human body is itself a composite individual, composed of multiple other individuals (bones and organs) which are composed of multiple other individuals (cells and micro-organisms), which are composed of multiple other individuals (molecules, protons, neurons), and so on. We can carry on identifying individuals down to the level of quarks and strings; future physics may take us further still.

It is only insofar as bodies communicate their motion to one another, and move at the same rate, that they compose one individual. All the elements of your body make up one individual because they communicate their motion to one another in a constant relation. If you have your appendix removed, it ceases to be part of you – not because it is spatially distinct from your body, but because it no longer communicates motion with your other bodily parts. The *identity* of an individual therefore depends on the constancy of the communication of motion between its parts and not on the parts themselves. That is how it is that individuals retain their identity even when their parts change, whether through their growth or diminishment (L4 and L5). A human being remains the same individual if her appendix is removed or has a blood transfusion. She remains the same individual over her whole life, despite the fact that every part of her will grow and change, and that some parts will disappear. An individual can be 'affected in many ways, and still preserve its nature' (L7S), so long as the communication of motion among its parts is constant.

So, individual bodies exist at multiple levels of compositional complexity. A fish is a composite individual; the river in which it swims is a bigger, multi-composite individual; the earth as a whole is a still bigger multi-composite individual, the galaxy bigger still; and all physical reality, finally, is one infinitely complex individual encompassing all the individuals within it. This infinitely complex individual is the infinite continuum of physicality. 'The whole of nature is one individual, whose parts, that is, all bodies, vary in infinite ways, without any change of the whole individual' (L7S).

What, then, can we say about the human body? It is 'composed of a great many individuals of different natures, each of which is highly composite' (Post. I). This high level of composition means that the human body is capable of doing a great many things and of being affected in very many ways (Post. III, Post. VI). The human body can move things and be moved by them; it can affect things and be affected by them; and it requires a great many other bodies (food, water, etc.) in order to continue being what it is (Post. IV). The complexity of the human body means that the human mind is correspondingly complex, and as a human body has more capabilities, its mind will be capable of perceiving more (P14). The human mind is 'composed of a great many ideas' corresponding to all the individuals that make up the body (P15).

The human mind is therefore capable of understanding a great many things. This explains why human minds are more capable of thinking than those of cats or caterpillars. It also suggests that if there are bodies in the universe that are more capable than human bodies, then there are minds that are more capable than ours of thinking. It seems to be Spinoza's view that no singular animal or object is more complex than a human being. However, Spinoza thinks there *are* individuals more complex than singular humans – not aliens (although that possibility is not ruled out), but *groups* of human beings, insofar as they move together as bigger, more complex individuals. We shall return to this in 'Part IV: Virtue, Ethics and Politics.'

Some questions arise from Spinoza's claim that where bodies are capable of doing more, minds are more capable of thinking. Does this mean that a disabled person has a lesser capacity to think than an able-bodied one? Does it mean that an Olympic runner has a greater thinking ability than a weak-bodied scientist? The answer to these questions is clearly 'no'. Each human body is highly complex in its own particular way, and each human mind thinks according to what its own body can do. The physical capability of the runner does not mean that he has a greater ability to think *in general*. It means that he is able, to a greater extent than others, to understand his legs' movements and his body's capacity for covering distance. The scientist is able, to a greater extent than others, to understand changes in matter, since her body has been trained to be more capable of detecting those changes. Similarly, a disabled person has different, not lesser, capabilities of body and mind. While a person with a physical disability cannot conceive the abilities of the body that she lacks, her body is capable of actions and feelings that an able-bodied person's is not, and her mind is correspondingly complex. A person who communicates through signing affects others, and is affected by them, in a different but equally complex way to those who speak; a person using a wheelchair has an ability to move that is more complex than that of an able-bodied walker. Spinoza is not proposing that physically able people are more intelligent than those who are physically less able. He is saying that the capabilities of the mind are parallel to the body's capabilities for acting and being affected.

The mind is limited in its understanding to *what the body is*. The human body is a mode in the attribute of extension; that means the human mind can understand *only* the attribute of extension, along with the attribute of thinking. This is why human minds cannot have knowledge of any of the infinite other attributes. Every finite mode is expressed through *all* the infinite attributes, but the human mind does not include ideas of what it itself *is* in these other attributes. The human mind is strictly the idea of a body in the attribute of extension. For that reason, our knowledge is limited to the realms of thinking and extension, and Spinoza is therefore unable to say anything about the infinite other attributes, beyond the logical necessity that they exist.

Sensation, Experience and Consciousness

Spinoza's explanation of bodily sensation is set out in Postulate V following L7. It is a minimal explanation and makes little sense without some background knowledge of Descartes' theory of vision. While Spinoza departs significantly from Descartes in his theory of experience, his understanding of the mechanics of sensation is largely Cartesian. In his *Optics* (1637), Descartes argued that the object of sensation – a tree, for instance – presses against and causes motion in our sense organs. Through constantly moving particles in the nerves, that motion is transmitted to the brain, causing an image of the tree to be physically 'impressed' on it. Descartes argued that, in this respect, seeing a tree is no different from touching it: the tree presses against the air, which presses against the eye.

Given Spinoza's claim that bodies are physically continuous, it makes sense that he would adopt Descartes' theory of sensation. The tree, the air, the eye and the brain are one continuous body, distinguished only by different rates of motion. The human body becomes aware of an external body through being affected by its motion. This happens when the external body determines 'a fluid part of the body' so that the fluid part 'frequently thrusts against a soft part of the body', changing the surface of the latter and impressing on it 'certain traces of the external body striking against the fluid part' (Post. V). A 'fluid part' is defined as a body whose parts are in motion (A3′), and presumably refers to the sense organs with their constantly moving particles. If that is right, then Spinoza is saying that the tree determines these particles to press frequently against the brain (the 'soft part' of the body) and to impress traces on it. Like Descartes, Spinoza sees no essential difference between sight, smell, taste, hearing and touch. All sensation involves this physical process: external things move against our senses, which impress images on the surface of our brains.

This account of sensation is no longer credible, but Spinoza's notion of the physicality of sensation is broadly acceptable. After all, the idea that external motions cause moving particles to press against the brain is not so very different from the theory that light photons hit the retina and cause it to produce neural impulses. We should not dismiss Spinoza's conception of experience merely on the grounds that his understanding of sensation is incorrect; rather, we should see whether his conception can work with our current theory of sensation. Spinoza would expect nothing less: if his theory of experience is right, then it will be compatible with any good scientific explanation.

Spinoza's theory of experience is based on the *traces* which result from the encounter between the moving particles of sensation (determined by an external object) and the brain. Reading Postulate

V carefully, we see that the traces impressed on the brain are not straightforwardly traces of the tree; they are traces of *the tree striking against the sense organs*. In other words, we do not have experience *of the tree*, but rather experience *of the tree as it affects our sense organs*. This is expressed in P16: the encounter between the human body and an external body involves the nature of the human body *and* the nature of the external body (see also A1′). So the particular way in which a body is affected will be determined by the nature of that body *and* by the nature of the body affecting it.

There is a parallel encounter between the ideas of those bodies that involves the nature of both ideas. Parallelism means that the mind is affected by the ideas of whatever the brain is physically affected with. So, as the brain is affected by the tree-determined sense organs, the mind is affected by the *idea* of the tree-determined sense organs. Because we constantly have experiences of external things affecting our sense organs, the human mind perceives the ideas of a great many external bodies, together with the idea of its own body (P16C1). The ideas that we have of external bodies are therefore always attached to the idea of our own body. Just as we do not have experience *of the tree*, our minds do not have the idea *of the tree*. We have the idea *of the tree as it affects our sense organs*. For this reason, 'the ideas we have of external bodies indicate the condition of our own body more than the nature of the external bodies' (P16C2). This also explains how it is that people understand the same object in different ways. Each person experiences the tree through his own sense organs and has ideas of the tree from the perspective of his own body.

You can see, then, that the senses cannot give us pure, 'objective' knowledge of things outside us, because our experience of external things always involves the 'subjective' experience of our own bodies at the same time. We cannot get outside our body in order to experience external things on their own. The external world is always experienced through the body and our empirical knowledge always involves ideas of our body.

As our experience of other things necessarily involves our own body, our experience of our own body necessarily involves other things. Our body is 'continually regenerated' by external things (e.g. the air that we breathe, the food that we eat), which means that the experience of external things is a necessary part of our existence.

We cannot have a purely inner consciousness of our bodies, isolated from the world we exist in. Rather, the existence and nature of our body are revealed to us only insofar as it is affected by other bodies and insofar as our mind has the ideas of those affections (P19). We are conscious of the body only through what it does and undergoes in the world.

Similarly, the mind is conscious of itself only insofar as it has 'ideas of ideas' of what goes on in the body (P23). 'Ideas of ideas' (P20) explain how we have thoughts *about* ideas in the mind. Since our minds are conscious of our bodies only insofar as they are affected, our thinking about our consciousness also refers to the body's affections. 'The mind does not know itself, except insofar as it perceives the ideas of the affections of the body' (P23).

We are self-conscious only insofar as we have ideas of our being affected by other things. The mind does not know itself as a *self*, but rather as a collection of ideas about what happens in and to the body. Insofar as we are finite modes, there is no pure knowledge of the self, no consciousness of an 'I think' that precedes our interactions in the world. It is, rather, the other way around. Self-consciousness depends on the body's interaction with other bodies and the mind's interaction with other ideas. Self-consciousness increases with our bodily capabilities. In this way, Spinoza anticipates the twentieth-century phenomenologist Maurice Merleau-Ponty (2002: 159): 'Consciousness is in the first place not a matter of "I think" but of "I can"'.

Imagining

Due to parallelism, experience is both bodily and mental. When you cut your finger with a knife, the experience involves the physical sharpness of the knife, the physical softness of your finger, the physical agitation of your sense organs (pain) and the physical trace of the knife–finger–pain encounter on your brain. In the parallel attribute of thinking, this encounter involves ideas of the knife, the finger and the pain, and the mental trace of the knife–finger–pain encounter on your mind.

These *traces* of the encounter remain, both physically on the brain and mentally in the mind, with the result that we continue to regard the external object as present to us unless those traces are destroyed by others (P17). Think of it this way: if your brain is impressed with traces of the knife encounter, then so long as those traces remain, that experience continues to be present to you. The experience remains 'present to mind' and is continually repeated when the 'fluid' sense organs *flow over* the traces which have been left on the brain. The movement with which those traces were first produced is thereby *repeated*, and thus the *sensation* of the external object is repeated too (P17C). Mentally, the idea of that sensation is repeated and the mind continues to regard the external object as present, even if it no longer exists.

Obviously, Spinoza is not saying that we continue to believe that the knife is cutting our finger, even after we have bandaged the finger and put the knife in a drawer. He is explaining how our experiences remain 'present to mind' after they have happened. The knife–finger–pain encounter has changed our body and mind, and *that change* continues to be present. The change leads us to repeat the encounter by thinking about it. To think about an experienced thing is to re-present it, to regard it as present to us.

The traces of ideas that are left in our minds from experience are called *images*. When the mind thinks about things insofar as they are, or have been, experienced, it *imagines* (P17S). Our minds are full of the images of our experience. These images are not 'snapshots' of external things; nor are they strictly visual. They are traces of the ideas of external things as they have affected your body, through seeing, hearing, touching, tasting or smelling. Your image of the knife–finger–pain encounter is specific to your experience. Each person therefore imagines, and associates images, in a way that reflects her own experience (P18).

Imagining encompasses experiencing, reflecting, remembering, anticipating, dreaming, hallucinating, representing, fictionalising and every other activity based on experience. Imagining therefore takes up an enormous amount of our mental activity. Memory is the connection of images according to the order in which our own bodies have been affected – which explains why people remember the same event differently, and why some aspects of an event are impressed on us more strongly than others (P18S). In imagination we anticipate the future and draw inferences, depending on how our experience has determined us to associate images. A Scottish farmer who has repeatedly experienced strong winds followed by rain will, upon feeling the wind, anticipate rain and a good harvest; a Thai fisherman who associates strong winds with tsunamis will fear destructive waves. Dreaming, too, is based on images. Since dreaming and experiencing are two forms of imagining, it is natural that we should confuse them from time to time and doubt whether our experience is real. Doubt is a necessary feature of imagining.

Imagining is not to be dismissed as mere fanciful dreaming or idle thoughts. A great deal of our knowledge is based on experience and is therefore 'imaginary'. This does not mean that it is false or fictional, but it does mean that it is uncertain. Since empirical knowledge is based on images, and since the association of images varies according to each person's experience, this kind of knowledge is subject to disagreement, doubt and revision. The farmer may have always experienced strong winds followed by rain, but he will not be certain that strong winds are *necessarily* followed by rain, so he will not be certain of the future. Some of our imaginings will turn out to be false: for centuries people imagined that the earth was flat, based on their experience of looking at the horizon. It was natural that people should have based this inference on the evidence of their senses, but that inference was never certain and had to be revised when science determined that the earth was spherical.

In other words, if *all* our knowledge were empirical, we would be unable to gain certainty about it (as Hume was later to argue). Fortunately, Spinoza says, there is another kind of knowledge. Our knowledge of the spherical shape of the earth is not based on our experience of looking at it. It is based on mathematical reasoning, where ideas are connected not according to the experiences of the body, but according to 'the order of the intellect, by which the mind perceives things through their first causes, and which is the same in all men' (P18S). This is the first indication Spinoza gives that there are two ways of knowing: the first through imagination, the second through reason. We shall return to this distinction in due course.

Essence and Existence

We now understand Spinoza's theory of experience. External things affect and leave traces on our bodies, and the ideas of those things affect and leave images in our minds. Since our bodies are inseparable from the physical world, we are constantly experiencing; and since we gain experience only through the body, our empirical knowledge of other things always involves the nature of our own body too. It seems that experiences are a necessary feature of our existence, preventing us from having pure, objective or certain knowledge, either of external things or of our own bodies.

Here is what we don't yet understand. If our necessary entanglement in the physical world makes pure, intuitive knowledge of our own bodies impossible, how can it *also* be true that the mind perceives everything that happens to the body (P12)? To reiterate the question that we asked earlier, if the mind is the idea of the body (P13), and if the mind has knowledge of everything that happens to the body (P12), then why is it that we understand so little of what actually goes on in our bodies? There seems to be a distinction between the mind's true and complete knowledge of the body on one level and its partial, empirical understanding of the body on another.

Your mind does indeed exist on two distinct 'levels'. *In its essence,* your mind is the true and complete idea of your body. But *in its finite existence,* your mind is the partial consciousness of your body's affectedness. The former is God's idea in the infinite intellect: here, the mind is not a finite mode, but part of an infinite mode. The *essence* of your mind is therefore to be part of the infinite intellect and to be the clear, distinct and complete idea of your body, as described in P12. But when it is expressed as an *actually existing finite mode,* your mind is expressed *along with* the other finite modes that you constantly interact with. Here, God actively conceives your mind together with 'a great many other ideas' (P19Dem). From God's perspective, each idea is conceived distinctly. But our finite minds are *being conceived* along with many other ideas, meaning that our own thinking is necessarily entangled with those other ideas. Your mind, in its finite existence, is *necessarily entangled with* the ideas of external things; in Spinoza's phrase, it is 'confused' with them.

As an example, take the experience you are having right now: the experience of reading this book. In essence, you and the book are distinct modes, the ideas of which exist distinctly in the infinite intellect. But in existence, you and the book are not distinct: your hands, eyes and brain are being physically affected and changed by the book, and your mind is being impressed with an image of the book's idea. This experience can be described as God conceiving your mind *together with* the idea of the book (see P11C); although God understands both you

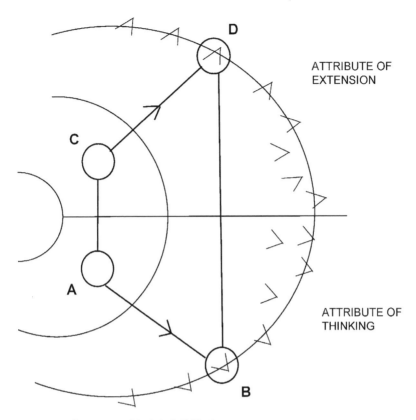

ATTRIBUTE OF
EXTENSION

ATTRIBUTE OF
THINKING

Figure 2.2 The structure of the finite individual

and the book clearly and distinctly, *you* cannot understand the nature of the book distinctly from your own senses, nor can you understand your body distinctly from the book you hold. Being a finite mode necessarily involves this physical and mental 'confusion' with other finite modes, and thus your finite mind cannot *exist as* the full, true, 'clear and distinct' idea of the body, which it is in its essence.

So, how do we exist at both of these 'levels' simultaneously? Figure 2.2 illustrates how our essence is *expressed* as our finite existence and how the human mind–body fits into the structure of reality as I explained it in 'Part I: Being, Substance, God, Nature.' (Figure 2.2 builds on Figure 1.5.)

ABDC represents one finite individual. It could be any individual, but let's imagine it is you, an existing human being. You are part of the infinite sphere of substance and are expressed across the attributes of thinking and extension. (You are also expressed through infinite other attributes, but for simplicity's sake they are neither represented nor discussed here.)

Point A is your mind's *essence*. It is in the 'infinite intellect' sector of the sphere, because it is part of the infinite intellect. Point B is your mind, insofar as it *exists* as a finite mode. B exists as one 'wave' on the surface of the continuum of existing ideas and it is constantly interacting with other finite ideas (i.e. it is constantly amassing images). Your mind's finite existence (B) is the *expression* of its essence (A), but B does not follow necessarily from A, since the essence of finite things does not include their existence (IP24). Instead, B is caused by God, insofar as God is expressed as the other finite things that causally determine it (IP28).

Your actually existing finite mind (B) is the idea of your actually existing finite body (D). As we saw in P7, the finite mind and the finite body are *the same thing*, understood now as a thinking mind, now as a physical body. But your finite body (D) is not caused by your finite mind (B), since there is no causality between attributes. Nor is your finite body the expression of your mind's essence (A). Rather, your finite body is a 'wave' on the surface of the continuum of physical bodies. As such, it is *expressed by* certain relations of motion and rest, relations which are part of the infinite mode of 'motion and rest'. There is a certain set of relations of motion and rest that pertains specifically to your body and that determines you as the individual that you are (see L1). That set of relations is represented by Point C. Your actual body (D) is not caused by C, for the same reason that B is not caused by A.

Point C can therefore be understood as the 'essence' of your body: the complete set of relations of motion that your body is capable of. Just as your actually existing mind (B) is the partial expression of its essence (A), 'confused' with many other ideas, your actually existing body (D) is the partial expression of *its* essence (C), 'confused' with many other bodies. Your finite body is constantly interacting with other finite bodies, some of which preserve your body, others of which decompose it. The bodily interactions that happen at D correspond to the images amassed at B.

A is therefore the true idea of C. The essence of your mind truly comprehends the relations of motion and rest that pertain to your body and truly comprehends all of your body's physical capabilities. Just as BD is *one being* understood through two attributes, AC is the single *essence* of that same being understood through two attributes (see P10C). The essence of the human being is therefore AC: this is the mind–body understood from God's perspective. The finite existence of the human being is BD: the mind–body insofar as it is a finite mode, bound up with other finite modes, and understood from our own perspective.

Adequate and Inadequate Knowledge

We now see that Spinoza's epistemology involves two perspectives: true understanding as it exists in God's infinite intellect and the partial understanding of the finite mode who is always bound up with experience and images. This is Spinoza's important distinction between *adequate and inadequate knowledge.*

What does Spinoza mean by the terms *adequate* and *inadequate*? In D4, Spinoza defined an *adequate idea* as an idea which, 'insofar as it is considered in itself, without relation to an object, has all the properties, or intrinsic denominations of a true idea'. So, what is a true idea? A true idea is God's activity of thinking, and all ideas are true insofar as they are God's (P32). Each idea in the infinite intellect is a true idea *of* some object (see IA6). But it is not their correspondence to an object that makes ideas true. Rather, it is the intrinsic truth of the ideas that allows us to understand their correspondence (P43S). Here is an example Spinoza gives to clarify this in his earlier text, the *Treatise on the Emendation of the Intellect:*

If an architect conceives a building in proper fashion, although such a building has never existed nor is ever likely to exist, his thought is nevertheless a true thought, and the thought is the same whether the building exists or not. On the other hand, if someone says, for example, that Peter exists, while yet not knowing that Peter exists, that thought in respect to the speaker is false, or, if you prefer, not true, although Peter really exists. The statement 'Peter exists' is true only in respect of one who knows for certain that Peter exists. (TEI 69, CW 19)

These examples perfectly illustrate how Spinoza's theory of truth differs from more contemporary theories. We tend to think that the statement 'Peter exists' is true if and only if Peter exists, and that the speaker has a true belief, even though he does not know that Peter exists. But for Spinoza, this statement is *not* true if it is made by someone who lacks true understanding of Peter's existence. The statement 'Peter exists' is true if and only if the idea of Peter's existence is fully and truly understood. The truth does not reside in the relation between the statement and the fact, but rather in the *full, active conceiving* of the idea in the infinite intellect. That is why the architect's *full conception* of a building is true, regardless of whether or not the building actually exists.

An adequate idea is an idea understood fully and truly: it is the activity of thought that is sufficient and necessary for understanding the idea completely. The adequate idea of any thing must include an understanding of its causes and of its determination through the necessity of the divine nature (IP29). To take the prime example, our true idea of God includes the conception of God's self-causing and its necessary existence (IP11). A true idea of a finite mode includes a full conception of the causes that determine it. Adequate ideas are not constructed by us; they exist in the infinite intellect, and when we understand adequately, we 'tap in' to the true thinking activity of the infinite intellect.

Since the human mind (A) is part of the infinite intellect, each human mind is itself an adequate idea, i.e. the true, full, active conceiving of the human body. So, in our essence, we have adequate understanding of ourselves. But insofar as we are finite modes, the human mind (B) does not have full access to that adequate understanding of its own body. Instead, the finite mind has partial, or *inadequate*, knowledge of its own body and similarly *inadequate* knowledge of the other bodies it interacts with. In the infinite intellect, every adequate idea is understood *clearly* and *distinctly* from the other adequate ideas. But when they are expressed as finite ideas all together, they are confused with one another, such that our own understanding of those same ideas is partial and indistinct, i.e. *inadequate*.

Given that finite existence necessarily involves 'confusion' with other things, we do not have adequate knowledge of external things, of our own bodies or our own minds (P24–9). For this reason, we do not have full knowledge of the causes or necessity of things; nor do we have adequate knowledge of things' duration in existence (P30–1). This means that from our finite perspective, 'all finite things are contingent and corruptible' (P31C). The notion that things are contingent – that they might have happened otherwise – is an *inadequate* understanding of reality, since in nature there is truly nothing contingent (IP29). Such misapprehensions are an inevitable aspect of being a finite mode.

This does not mean that all inadequate knowledge is entirely untrue. It means that inadequate knowledge is *uncertain*, as we have already seen. Inadequate ideas are fragments of full, adequate ideas. This means that every inadequate idea involves some truth. But every inadequate idea also involves the *privation* of truth and therefore falsity (P35). Falsity has no positive being (P33); it is simply the incompleteness and confusedness that all ideas involve when they are inadequately understood. So the statement 'Peter exists', when said by someone who does not *know* that Peter exists, is false only in the sense that it is inadequately understood. The speaker has not gained true understanding of Peter's existence; when he does, his uncertain belief will be true knowledge.

For Spinoza, it is impossible to have a *true belief* that is not *knowledge*. Either you have an uncertain belief, which therefore involves falsity, or you have true knowledge. Error, then, is an inherent aspect of being a finite mode who is necessarily implicated in the world. Insofar as we experience and imagine, we are bound to err.

Common Notions

It is important to understand that for Spinoza, 'the truth is out there'. True ideas really do exist in the infinite intellect. Our minds are *essentially* modes of true understanding, and in its essence, the mind understands the body adequately. The question is, can we ever access this truth and regain the adequate understanding of our own bodies that is lost to us as finite modes? Our adequate self-knowledge is obscured by our constant encounters with things that clutter our minds with inadequate ideas and prevent us from conceiving our own body clearly and distinctly. It seems that our true knowledge is severely limited by the nature of finite existence.

I say expressly that the mind has, not an adequate, but only a confused [and mutilated] knowledge, of itself, of its own body, and of external bodies, so long as it perceives things from the common order of Nature, that is, so long as it is determined externally, from fortuitous encounters with things, to regard this or that, and not so long as it is determined internally, from the fact that it regards a number of things at once, to understand their agreements, differences, and oppositions. For so often as it is disposed internally, in this or another way, then it regards things clearly and distinctly, as I shall show below. (P29S)

Insofar as we gain knowledge from our 'fortuitous encounters' in experience – that is, through imagination – we understand things partially and confusedly. But there is also the potential for that other kind of knowledge that Spinoza referred to in P18S: knowledge that does not depend on experiences, but on reason. With this second kind of knowledge, the mind understands things 'clearly and distinctly', i.e. adequately and truly. This adequate knowledge comes about from our 'regarding a number of things at once', in terms of their 'agreements, differences and oppositions'. This is Spinoza's doctrine of the *common notions*.

Back at L2, Spinoza had demonstrated that all bodies agree in certain things. All physical bodies are understood through the attribute of extension, and all physical bodies involve motion and rest. At P38 Spinoza argues that 'those things which are common to all, and which are equally in the part and in the whole, can only be conceived adequately'. This suggests that we necessarily have adequate knowledge of those things that all bodies agree in: extension, and motion and rest.

How does this work? Consider *extension* as something that is common to all bodies: all bodies are modes of the attribute of extension. In order to fully understand what a body is, we need to understand the nature of extension. That means that the adequate idea of every body *involves* the adequate idea of extension. Your mind, as the true idea of your body, therefore involves the true idea of extension. And the 'minds' or true ideas of the bodies you interact with involve that same true idea of extension. Now when your body encounters another body – when you sit on a chair, for instance – the bodies interact and the ideas are confused together; your ideas of the chair

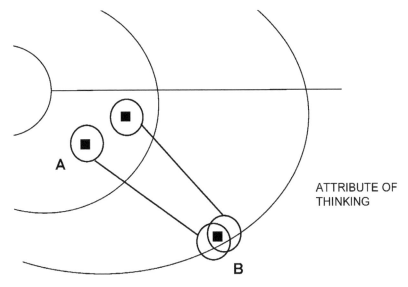

Figure 2.3 Acquiring common notions

and the body are inadequate. But the adequate idea of *extension*, which is common to both ideas, is not confused in this encounter. Instead, it is clarified. This is because the true idea of extension *that is already part of your mind* is reinforced by the same true idea that is part of the idea of the chair. Extension as such is not apprehended through the senses, and the mind does not perceive it as an image. Instead, through the encounter you *recover* a true idea that was immanent to both you and the chair.

Figure 2.3 illustrates your mind (B) interacting with the idea of the chair and clarifying an idea that your mind has in its essence (A). (The body is, of course, parallel to the mind, but for simplicity's sake it has not been illustrated here).

Extension is what Spinoza calls a 'common notion' (P40S1). Extension can *only* be conceived adequately because it is immanent to *all* things. And the more encounters we have with other bodies, the clearer this idea of extension becomes. You may think that you do not actually have a very clear idea of what extension is. But Spinoza claims that you do, and the evidence for this is in the things that you know with certainty. When you pull out a chair to sit on it, you know with certainty that the chair will not suddenly disappear. When a ball rolls down a hill, you know with certainty that you will have to increase your velocity to catch up with it. You don't need to doubt the basic properties of physical being, because you truly understand some aspects of the nature of extension and motion and rest; those aspects that your body has in common with other bodies. From position B, you have tapped in to some of the true knowledge about yourself that is included in point A.

Common notions exist at different levels of commonality. Some, like extension, are common to all bodies. Others, such as the capacity for self-propulsion, are common only to certain types of bodies. Others, such as the capacity to walk on two legs, are common only to human bodies (P39). Insofar as the body has something in common with other bodies, the mind's idea of that common feature will be reinforced and our mind will recover the adequate idea of that feature. Gaining adequate ideas is a process of *recovering* the true idea of the body: through encounters with things that we have something in common with, we begin to recover the truth of ourselves.

A number of consequences follow from the doctrine of common notions. First, bodies that have more things in common with other bodies will be more capable of forming common notions (P39C). This means that bodies that are more complex and capable of more interactions have minds that are more capable of regaining adequate ideas. Second, we will be better able to gain adequate ideas by interacting more with things that have something in common with us. Interacting with other people is a surer route to adequate knowledge than interacting with animals or machines. We will return to the social and political implications of this fact in 'Part IV: Virtue, Ethics and Politics.'

The common notions are a pathway to adequate knowledge, because adequate ideas lead to more adequate ideas (P40). Once it is truly understood, the adequate idea of motion and rest leads the mind to understand certain properties of moving bodies (such as the ones Spinoza sets out in A1' and A2' after P13). So once we have one adequate idea, we are capable of truly understanding the ideas that follow from it. In fact, we can see the *Ethics* as one long chain of adequate ideas that started with the adequate idea of 'cause of itself' (ID1).

It is important to note that common notions are not general

concepts, or what Spinoza calls 'transcendental' and 'universal' terms (P40S1). Terms such as 'thing', 'dog' and 'building' arise because our minds become so crowded with images of particular things, dogs and buildings that all those particulars become confused with one another. As a result, the mind imagines them without any distinction, under a general term which refers to none of them in particular. Since they are generalised images of the multiple images that come to us in experience (images of images), these universals are very inadequately understood: they 'signify ideas that are confused in the highest degree' (P40S1). A common notion, by contrast, is a property that is truly shared by particular bodies. Common notions are not known through images; they are known because their truth is already included in our essence. Our encounters with other bodies make possible the revelation of these true ideas that were always already part of what we are.

The Three Kinds of Knowledge

We now understand the difference between inadequate knowledge based on images and adequate knowledge based on the common notions. This is Spinoza's distinction between imagination and reason. These are two of three kinds of knowledge available to us. Spinoza sets these out in the second scholium to P40.

The first kind of knowledge is **imagination**, opinion or empirical knowledge. This is confused and uncertain knowledge based on inadequate ideas. Such knowledge comes to us in a number of ways. As we have seen, a great deal of it comes to us through our sense-perceptions and the images that result from them: those images are organised into memories, anticipations, inferences, and so on. Since these imaginings depend on what we happen to encounter through our senses, Spinoza calls it 'knowledge from random experience' (P40S2).

The ideas that we form from signs and language are similarly inadequate. The fact that reading or hearing the word 'apple' makes us think of an apple is a variety of imagining. For the thing has no intrinsic relation to the articulate sound and has 'nothing in common with it except that the body of the same man has often been affected by these two at the same time, that is, that the man often heard the word [apple] while he saw the fruit' (P18S). For Spinoza, truth does not reside in words or statements. Words, signs and sentences are images that *represent* true ideas, so words alone can only ever give us imaginary knowledge. (In reading the *Ethics*, however, you are looking at words and building true understanding simultaneously.)

The second kind of knowledge is **reason**, knowledge 'from the fact that we have common notions and adequate ideas of the properties of things' (P40S2). Knowledge based on reason is necessarily true, because insofar as we have such knowledge, we access adequate ideas as God has them (P41). To have true knowledge is to *know* that we have true knowledge: understanding a thing fully and truly *includes* the true understanding that you understand it. 'Truth is its own standard', Spinoza says (P43S), and true knowledge teaches us to distinguish truth from falsity (P42). Rational knowledge, then, enables us to understand the limitations and errors of imagination.

As we have already seen, a true idea includes an understanding of that thing's causes and its necessity in the divine nature. When we know rationally, then, we understand how things have come about and that they are necessary, not contingent (P44). It is only when we imagine that we regard things as contingent and that we regard future events as possibilities. When we understand through reason, we know truly that nothing is contingent and that everything that has happened and that will happen has been necessarily determined (IP29).

Gaining reason involves building up common notions, i.e. clarifying ideas that are already part of the essence of our minds. Gaining rational knowledge, then, means regaining the truth that our minds fundamentally are. As we become more rational, we get back on track with our mind's essential activity of true understanding – the activity that happens at point A. Through reason we gain better understanding of ourselves and our place in the universe.

But reason is not something we are born with; it must be built up and developed, through the common notions that we gain in our encounters in the world. It is only by *having experiences* with other bodies that we will build up these common notions and become more rational. So, although Spinoza believes empirical knowledge to be the source of falsity, he does not believe that experience is worthless. Quite the contrary, for without experiential encounters with other

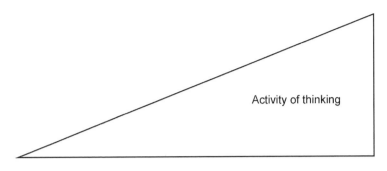

More imagination   More rational knowledge

Figure 2.4 Imagination and reason

bodies, we would never build up the common notions that enable us to become rational. Indeed, we must seek to encounter a wide variety of other things, experiment with them and learn about them, in our search for common notions and rational knowledge. We develop rational knowledge *through* experience and imagination.

Imagination and reason, then, are not opposed to one another. Just as an inadequate idea is an adequate idea that is fragmented and confused, imagination is rational knowledge that is partial, confused and uncertain. Every human being has both kinds of knowledge, in differing degrees. It is impossible to be wholly imaginative, since *every* mind truly understands the very basic properties of extension (see P45–47); and it is impossible to be wholly rational, since every mind is a finite mode that necessarily interacts with others. Each person's mind, or *activity of thinking*, is always in some position on a continuum of imagination and reason as shown in Figure 2.4.

In P40S2 Spinoza also speaks of a third kind of knowledge: **intuition**. At this point, it is not clear what is meant by this, nor how this knowledge relates to the other two kinds. We do not get clarity about the third kind of knowledge until Part V of the *Ethics*. We shall therefore put it to one side until we get to 'Part V: Freedom and Eternity'. For the time being, focus on the two kinds of knowledge that you know your mind to be capable of: imagination and reason.

The Denial of Free Will

We learned in Part I that the universe is fully determined and that there is no free will. Spinoza now states this point explicitly, arguing that since the mind is a mode of thinking, it cannot determine itself freely (P48). This means that there is no absolute faculty of willing, that is, no part of the mind which acts autonomously from other parts of the mind. When Spinoza argues that there is no free will, he means that no part of the mind can be the absolute causal origin of an effect. Every part of the mind is determined by other modes of thinking.

Our inadequate knowledge of ourselves, of the necessity of our actions and of the *causes* that determine us mean that we imagine ourselves to be free. Because we act without knowing the causes of our actions, we imagine our volitions to be their cause. Spinoza illustrates this nicely in Letter 58. He asks his reader to imagine a stone which is pushed to roll down a hill; like the stone, our physical actions are physically determined. Next, he goes on,

Conceive, if you please, that while continuing in motion the stone thinks, and knows that it is striving, as far as it can, to continue in motion. Now this stone, since it is conscious only of its striving and is not at all indifferent, will surely think it is completely free, and that it continues in motion for no other reason than it so wishes. This, then, is that human freedom which all men boast of possessing, and which consists solely in this, that men are conscious of their desire and unaware of the causes by which they are determined. (CW 909, translation modified)

We cannot appeal to the difference between human beings and stones in order to claim that we are free, even if the stone is not. Stones too have minds and desires (albeit very simple ones), and Spinoza utterly denies that our minds are any more free than that of the stone. There are neither freely caused bodily actions nor freely caused thoughts.

Volitions are nothing other than modes of thinking, or ideas, that are part of the mind (P49C Dem.), and thus they must be fully determined; but we *imagine* that they issue from a faculty which can cause action by itself. The will is therefore not an independent faculty which freely chooses the ideas of the intellect to which it assents (as Descartes believed). Rather, 'the will and the intellect are one and the same' (P49C). When we seem to 'will' something, we are really just affirming a true idea or denying a false one; something that we are determined to do by the nature of true ideas (P48S, P49S). True ideas include knowledge of their truth, and thus cause us both to affirm them and to deny the truth of the false ones.

The long scholium to P49 is a rebuttal to the Cartesians. Descartes believed that the will freely chooses which ideas to assent to and that the will is the source of error in that it sometimes assents to ideas that are not clear and distinct. By contrast, Spinoza believes there can be no choice about assenting to true ideas and no possibility of truly assenting to false ones. Error is not a positive action of the mind; it is simply the truth-privation that inadequate ideas involve. Spinoza offers numerous examples of erroneous judgements in P49S to illustrate these points.

What can we know? We can gain true knowledge of the adequate ideas that are part of our essence. We gain true knowledge in two ways: through experience, in which common notions are clarified; and through reasoning, where we deduce from one adequate idea the adequate ideas that follow from it. Human beings, therefore, are capable of knowing a great deal. Since everything in the attributes of thinking and extension has something in common with us, we can know a great deal about our world, and we know more about it as we explore it and discover its workings. Since our minds are essentially the full adequate idea of our bodies, we can know a great deal about ourselves, too. Gaining true knowledge is a matter of regaining adequate ideas of our own bodies. Becoming more rational is a project of reconnecting with our essential minds and recovering true knowledge of our own nature. This is not an introspective exercise that can be achieved by thinking alone. We must seek to encounter things in the world, to share knowledge with others and to increase our body's capabilities of acting. Becoming more rational, and knowing ourselves, involves becoming more active, both physically and mentally.

Part III: The Affects

Part III, 'On the Origin and Nature of the Affects', is about how we are *affected* by things. Affects are the feelings and desires that arise in us as a result of our encounters and experiences: affects push and pull us in different directions, determining our actions and behaviour, sometimes overwhelming us. Affects are also known as *passions*, because we are passive to the things that affect us.

The passions had been discussed in philosophical discourse before, usually as bodily phenomena that were contrary to reason and needed to be overcome. In *The Passions of the Soul* (1649), Descartes diagnoses the physical mechanics of feeling and argues that a strong will, guided by reason, can gain mastery over the passions. Spinoza agrees that the passions are non-rational: they arise in experience and are therefore related to imaginative knowledge. But Spinoza pointedly refuses to mock or denigrate the passions. Our feelings are *part of nature* and follow with the same necessity as other things. A human being is not 'a dominion within a dominion' that can determine himself regardless of the order of nature (III Pref.). Having feelings does not indicate weakness of will; it does indicate that things in nature have the power to affect us, sometimes very forcefully. We should not ignore or repress the passions. Since we are necessarily subject to them, we should try to understand them and their causes as clearly as we can.

Part III is dedicated to looking at *how we are determined by* our experiences. It is a diagnosis of what it is to be a finite mode, constantly interacting with other finite modes – not on the level of knowledge, but on the level of feeling. Since feelings come about in experience, they are closely connected to imaginative knowledge. Indeed, Spinoza defines the affects as 'confused ideas' (Gen. Def. Aff.), just like images. Let us see why this is.

Activity and Passivity

In the first definition of Part III, Spinoza introduces a distinction between *adequate* and *inadequate causes*. This is similar to the distinction between adequate and inadequate knowledge that we looked at in the last section, but it refers to the way our minds and bodies cause effects.

Due to parallelism (IIP7), the mind's activity and the body's activity are the same thing, understood in two ways. When the mind understands adequately, it has a true idea of some part of the body: an idea that is part of the nature of the mind and is not confused with ideas of other things. Parallel to the mind's activity of clearly understanding some part of body is the body's activity of clearly acting through that part. This activity is part of its nature and is not confused with bodies of other things. As the adequate idea in the mind causes other adequate ideas to follow from it, so too does one bodily activity *adequately cause* other bodily activities. Adequate knowledge is the mind's thinking activity that comes from its nature alone and is *fully the cause* of more true thinking activity. Similarly, adequate causation involves the body's physical activity being *fully the cause* of other physical activity. The effects can be clearly and distinctly understood through our body alone as cause. When we are the adequate cause of an effect, we are said to *act*; that is, 'when something in us or outside us follows from our nature, which can be clearly and distinctly understood through it alone' (D2).

We know from Part II, however, that most of our knowledge is inadequate and involves the nature of other things. So, too, most of our causality is inadequate, involving the nature of other things. Just as inadequate knowledge is confused and involves several partial ideas mixed together, an inadequate cause is the *partial cause* of an effect: the effect cannot be understood through that cause alone. When the mind is affected by the ideas of the things it experiences, those external ideas *act on* the mind and cause it to imagine. Similarly, when the body is affected by external things, those things act on the body and cause it to do things. When we are acted on by external things, we are only the partial cause of the effects that follow from us. Those effects follow both from our own nature, and from the nature of the external things, and we are the *inadequate cause* of the effects.

The body constantly interacts with other things which change and affect it. Some of those interactions preserve the body and enhance its ability to act; others decompose the body and obstruct it from acting fully. The ways in which external things enhance or obstruct our body's activity – and, in parallel, the ways in which the ideas of those things enhance or obstruct our mind's activity – are the ways in which external things *affect* us. The affects are the 'affections', or *changes*, of the finite body by which its power of acting is increased or diminished (D3). Eating an apple, for instance, affects us by giving us vitamins which enhance the body's constitutive relation, increasing its ability to act. Ingesting a poison, however, imparts destructive chemicals to the body which decompose its constitutive relation and diminish its ability to act. When we are acted on by external things we are passive to them and our affects are *passions*. When we cause our own bodily changes from our nature alone, then the affects are actions (D3).

This distinction between 'passive affects' (passions) that are caused inadequately and 'active affects' (actions) that are caused adequately is made clearer in P1 and P3. The more adequate ideas the mind has, the more it acts, and the more inadequate ideas it has, the more it is acted on. You can see why this is: inadequate ideas confuse the mind and affect it with images. They act on the mind, they change it and they cause it to imagine, just as the things act on and change our bodies. When you eat an apple, you feel an increase in your ability to act, both bodily and mentally, which follows both from your nature and from the nature of the apple. But your physical interaction with the apple is inadequately caused and inadequately understood: it is something you *undergo*. The resulting increase of your ability to act is not in your control. It is a passive affect.

By contrast, when the mind has adequate ideas, it perceives some aspect of the body fully and truly understands the effects that follow from it. In that case, effects follow from the mind alone. For example, as we saw in 'Part II: Minds, Bodies, Experience and Knowledge', you truly understand the extendedness of your body. From that adequate idea follows the adequate understanding of your ability to move yourself. From your mind follows the adequate idea of your body's self-propulsion and the nature of your body is the adequate cause of moving itself. Moving yourself is something you *do*, from the nature of your body alone. The resulting increase of your body's ability to act has been caused by you; it is an active affect.

From this follows something very important: 'the mind is more liable to passions the more it has inadequate ideas, and conversely, is more active the more it has adequate ideas' (P1C). The more the mind has encounters, amasses images and imagines, the more it will be affected by the things it encounters and the more passions it will feel. The more the mind regains common notions, thinks rationally and understands truly the nature of its body, the more the body will be able to cause its own actions and the more active it will be.

The Denial of Intentions

When we are acted on by other things and are the inadequate cause of our actions, other things partially determine what we do and say and how we feel and behave. The body is determined in its activity by other bodies, and the mind is determined in its thinking activity by their ideas. Spinoza reminds us here that the body cannot determine the mind and that the mind cannot determine the body (P2).

This point follows from IIP7, Spinoza's parallelism thesis. Spinoza reminds us of it here as a riposte to Descartes, who believes that the body causes the passions of the mind, and that the mind is capable of determining the body to be less affected by passions. For Spinoza, the body does not *cause* the mind to feel things and the mind cannot control the passions of the body. But where are the passions located: in the mind or in the body? Spinoza believes that the passions are both bodily and mental, because bodily passions *are* mental passions, expressed in a different attribute. The affects are felt both by the body and by the mind: 'the order of actions and passions of our body is, by nature, at one with the order of actions and passions of the mind' (P2S).

P2 reveals that our belief that we act intentionally is as ill founded as our belief in free will. There can be no intentional acts, because no mental event can cause a bodily event. All physical things and events exist through strictly physical causes and must be explained with reference to physical causes alone.

It is worth reminding ourselves of just how incredible this claim is. On Spinoza's account, our minds and ideas do not cause the movement of our bodies, our behaviour or our speech. Skilled activities such as flying a plane, writing computer code and performing heart surgery do not involve mental causation either. Beethoven's symphonies, Shakespeare's tragedies, the pyramids of Egypt and the Universal Declaration of Human Rights were not the result of ideas or thinking minds; these and all other human productions were caused through strictly physical means. Even reading, writing and discussing philosophy are physical activities with physical causes.

Spinoza expects our incredulity at his materialism. But he thinks that assigning mental causes to physical effects, as Descartes does, is far less credible, because it is incoherent. Descartes is unable to explain how the mind directs the body, for the simple reason that the mind does not direct the body. Instead of futilely trying to explain mental intentions, we should seek better knowledge of the laws of motion and rest to give us better understanding of the causes of things. The human body is highly complex and we do not have adequate knowledge of its capabilities or of the causes that determine it to act. Intentions are a fiction, like free will, which people appeal to in their ignorance of the true causes of their actions. To those who say that only an intentional mind can explain the production of a symphony or a pyramid, Spinoza simply says that 'they do not know what the body can do, or what can be deduced from the consideration of its nature alone' (P2S).

Similarly, our bodily actions are not in the free power of our minds, and nor are the words that we speak. Our minds do not freely choose or intend what we do or say. We are no different from 'the madman, the chatterbox, [and] the child, [who] believe that they speak from a free decision of the mind, when really they cannot contain their impulse to speak' (P2S).

Certainly, the mind makes decisions, but they are not *free* decisions. Our decisions are determined by our desires. That is why Spinoza says that decisions are really *appetites* that 'vary as the disposition of the body varies' (P2S). Determined by the appetite to eat an apple, the mind 'decides' to eat the apple and the body is physically determined to do so. But the decision does not cause the determination, because they are *the same appetite* expressed through the attributes of thinking and extension.

Conatus and Essential Desires

The next question is, where do these desires, or appetites, come from? What causes a finite mode to want certain things and to avoid others? Take hunger, the desire for food. Insofar as hunger is expressed physically, it must be caused by a physical cause. But hunger is not *caused* by the food in front of us. The body itself desires food instinctually. This desire seems to arise from a basic drive to life that inheres in every living being.

This basic drive to life is what Spinoza introduces in P6: it is a thing's *striving to persevere in its own being*, and this striving does indeed determine our basic desires. 'Striving' is Curley's translation of the Latin word *conatus*. 'Conatus' is used by early modern philosophers, including Thomas Hobbes (a major influence on Spinoza), to express the notion of a thing's endeavour for what is advantageous to it. Like

Hobbes, Spinoza believes conatus drives all things in nature. Each thing, as far as it can by its own power, strives to persevere in its being (P6). The neurologist Antonio Damasio believes that conatus is equally explicable as 'the aggregate of dispositions laid down in brain circuitry that . . . seeks both survival and well-being' (Damasio 2004: 36). We strive to carry on living and flourishing. We naturally desire those things that further our life's flourishing, and we try to avoid those things that threaten or diminish it.

How should we understand conatus in terms of Spinoza's metaphysics? Recall that as modes of God, all things express God's *power* or God's self-actualising activity. Each finite mode expresses the power of God in a limited degree. The *essence* of a finite mode is to be a mode of God's infinite power: in the attribute of thinking, *the essence of your mind* is to be a mode of God's thinking activity, and in the attribute of extension, *the essence of your body* is to be a mode of God's activity of motion and rest. As finite modes, we *actualise* a degree of God's thinking and physical power and *we strive to carry on actualising it.* There is no further 'reason' why we strive to actualise God's power; as modes of God, that is simply what we do.

This power by which we strive, a degree of God's power, is our essence (P7). In other words, our essence is a drive for continued being. From our essence follows both our striving to persevere in our being and the determination to act in ways that satisfy that striving. As finite modes, then, we are *essentially determined* to carry on living and being what we are and to do those things that will enhance our life's flourishing. 'Instinctual' desires for survival, food, water, shelter, and so on, are determined by our essence. Our essence determines us to act in ways that will ensure our survival, promote our well-being and satisfy those desires.

As we strive to persevere in our being, we resist external things of a contrary nature that have the power to diminish and destroy our life's flourishing. Our eventual death will come about through this kind of destruction: for Spinoza, death always comes from the outside. Even natural death from ageing is externally imposed, as the constitutive relations between body parts break down due to environmental pressures. Death involves the irremediable decomposition of a body's constitutive relation by a body of a contrary nature and the accompanying decomposition of its mind by that body's idea (P5,

P10, P11S). A thing's essence cannot include anything that brings about its own destruction (P4). The Freudian idea of a 'death drive' would be utterly incoherent to Spinoza: it is impossible that a being should desire its own death. (We shall address the problem of suicide later.)

The *essence* of each thing, then, is conatus, the striving to persevere in its being; conatus is what makes each particular thing what it is. What it is to be this apple is to strive to carry on being this apple; what it is to be that horse is to strive to carry on being that horse. 'To be' an apple, a horse or a human being, then, is never a static state. It is the constant activity of being, or actualising, what you are. Because the human mind is self-conscious, it is conscious of its own striving (P9). This mental consciousness of striving is what we call will, but when striving is related to the mind and body together, it is called appetite. There is no difference between appetite and desire, except that desire involves consciousness of our appetite (P9S, see also Def. Aff. I).

This appetite, therefore, is nothing but the very essence of man, from whose nature there necessarily follow those things that promote his preservation. And so man is determined to do those things. (P9S)

Spinoza then makes an intriguing remark. From all this, he says, it is clear that we do not desire anything because we judge it to be good. On the contrary, we judge something to be good *because we desire it* (P9S). When our desires are determined by our essence, we necessarily strive for that which is good for the preservation of our own being. It can't be the case that we judge something to be good and then strive for it on the basis of that judgement. Rather, from our own nature, we strive for what is good for us, forming the basis for our judgement of what is good. We shall discuss that idea in detail in 'Part IV: Virtue, Ethics and Politics'.

Joy, Sadness and Imaginary Desires

When our essential desires are satisfied, our survival is furthered and our well-being increases; but when those desires are frustrated, our survival diminishes and our well-being decreases. In other words, the satisfaction of our striving affects us positively and increases our ability to act, whereas the frustration of our striving affects us negatively and decreases our ability to act. Affects are the finite mode's *transitions* to greater or lesser power (see Def. Aff. III). These transitions are the waxing and waning of our very essence, also described as passages to greater and lesser perfection (P11S). 'Perfection' is not a value judgement; it refers to the amount of being a thing has. When we feel good, our being swells; when we feel bad, our being shrinks.

The mind's transition to greater perfection and flourishing is the passion of **joy**, and its transition to lesser perfection and flourishing is the passion of **sadness** (P11S). The parallel feelings of the body are pleasure and pain: pleasure increases our body's ability to act, whereas pain decreases it. Our feelings are the barometer of the well-being that we desire to enhance. Joy-pleasure increases the flourishing of our being, making the mind and body more active, and sadness-pain diminishes our flourishing and our activity. Desire, joy and sadness are the three 'primary affects' that are the basis of all our other feelings.

At our most basic, then, we desire things and we feel passions of joy and sadness, brought about by external things. That is, we are *acted on* by external things and their nature affects us, either towards an increase of our power or towards a decrease of it. Naturally enough, we strive to imagine things that increase our power – that is, to keep the experience of those things present to mind (P12). Similarly, we strive to exclude the presence of things that decrease our power (P13). This explains what **love** and **hatred** are: joy and sadness with the accompanying image of an external cause. When we love, we strive to have present to us the thing we imagine causes our joy; when we hate, we strive to remove or destroy the thing we imagine causes our sadness (P13S).

The passions depend on inadequate ideas and images (P3). We organise and associate images based on our particular experiences, and we associate feelings with images in the same way. There is nothing rational about the association of joy or sadness with a particular image, and there is nothing rational about love and hatred. Our feelings of love or hatred for a thing depend on happenstance: how a thing affected us when we first encountered it, whether we associate it with another thing that we love or hate, whether it resembles another thing that we love or hate, and so on (P14–17). 'Anything can be the accidental cause of joy, sadness, or desire', even if it has not caused that joy, sadness or desire itself (P15). A single bad experience with a dog leads someone to hate dogs; another person is drawn to people who resemble his first love; and we tend to desire things that we believe bring joy to others.

P15 indicates something important about desire: it too can be a passive affect, determined by experiences, images and chance associations. We saw earlier that desires for what preserves our being are determined by our essence. But we also have desires for things that do not preserve our being, such as a desire for nicotine or a desire to visit Peru. These desires have nothing to do with our striving to persevere in our being and are not determined by our essence. Instead, just like joy and sadness, they are determined by the experiences we have had, the images we have built up and our associations of images with feelings.

Affects are seldom simple and straightforward, as P17 shows. Since the body is composed of a great many individuals, each of which can be affected in numerous ways, one external body can affect it in many different and contrary ways. Add to this that we may associate images with contrary affects, and it frequently happens that something affects us with both sadness and joy, in which case 'we shall hate it and at the same time love it' (P17). Being affected by contrary affects is **vacillation of mind**, which is equivalent to doubt. If your consumption of red wine is followed as often by a headache as by a feeling of exuberance, then on any given occasion you will not be able to anticipate which will happen: your imagination will vacillate and you will doubt the future (IIP44S). Similarly, you will both hate and love red wine and you will be uncertain if it will bring you sadness or joy. Feelings of vacillation relate mostly to the future and are most apparent in **fear** and **hope** (P18S2).

The middle section of Part III (P18–52) sees Spinoza setting out different combinations of joy, sadness and desire, and considering how they are associated with different images to produce the specific affects that we feel. These propositions offer fascinating, recognisable diagnoses of human emotions, and it is in this section that we see Spinoza at his most personal. You may be surprised at just how relevant Spinoza's explanations are to your own experiences of feelings and human behaviour.

Note how often Spinoza uses the word 'imagine' in these propositions. This reminds us that our feelings depend on how things affect us in our encounters. It is insofar as we interact with other bodies that we feel the affects, so our affects are social and interpersonal in nature. Our feelings depend on how we *imagine* those interactions, in experience, memory and anticipation, and through resemblance and association. The passions are 'confused ideas' (Gen. Def. Aff.) that determine the majority of our feelings, thoughts and behaviour.

Affects of Sympathy and Antipathy

Our affects of joy and sadness vary with what we imagine to be the affects of the things we love and hate. That means our own feelings depend to a large extent on how others *seem to us* to be feeling and on what *seems to us* to be the cause of that feeling. The joy we feel at a thing we love is increased if we imagine that that thing feels joy and passes to a greater perfection: we feel increasing joy as we imagine the being of that thing increasing, since the mind's striving to imagine that thing is aided (P21). Our joy is decreased if we imagine that thing to feel sadness and to pass to a lesser perfection. Similarly, we feel love or hatred towards the imagined cause of joy or sadness in the thing that we love (P22). The inverse applies to a thing that we hate: we feel joy at his sadness and sadness at his joy. This explains affects of **envy** and ***Schadenfreude***, the pleasure we take in another's misfortune (P23–4).

Naturally, we strive to imagine those things that we imagine bring joy to us and to those we love and to exclude those things that we imagine bring sadness (P25). (Again, the inverse applies to those we hate.) But because this is based on what we *imagine* to cause joy or sadness, it can happen that we affirm and deny things to a greater extent than is just. If our imagining that we ourselves bring joy to those around us causes us disproportionately to strive to affirm our image of ourselves, we feel **pride**. If we strive disproportionately to negate the image of someone who we imagine to be the cause of our sadness, we feel **scorn** for that person (P26S).

Our affects depend heavily on our images of the feelings of other people. We are strongly affected by our images of how others feel, to the extent that even if we have no particular feelings towards someone, we will tend to be affected with the same feeling that seems to affect them (P27). Every experience involves the nature of our body and the nature of the other body (IIP16). If the nature of the other body is like our own, and provided that a stronger affect of hatred does not intervene, our image will involve the other body's feelings, which become confused with our image of our own body's feelings. The feelings of other people are integral to how we experience them and integral to how we are affected by them. So, when we *imagine* someone to feel a certain way, 'this imagination will express an affection of our body like this affect' (P27 Dem.). Our 'imitation' of the feelings we imagine others to have explains our feelings of **pity** and **emulation** (P27S). We feel sadness when we see others suffer; we love and hate what others love and hate; and we desire to have those things that others also desire.

Our images of how others feel about us is another important determinant of our feelings. We strive to do whatever we imagine others find pleasing; we **praise** those who we imagine to do those things and **blame** those who we imagine do not (P29, P29S). Our **kindness** towards others can easily become **ambition** when we do things solely from a desire to please others and to be praised by them. We **esteem** ourselves when we imagine we have done what others praise, and we feel **shame,** or **repentance,** when we imagine that we have done what others blame (P30). In these cases we feel joy or sadness accompanied by the image of ourselves as cause; so esteem is self-love and repentance is self-hatred (P30S). Since self-love is based on our imagining that we cause joy in others, 'it can easily happen that one who exults at being esteemed is proud and imagines himself to be pleasing to all, when he is burdensome to all' (P30S). Probably you know people like this, and presumably Spinoza did too.

Compassion, envy and ambition all stem from the same fact about human nature: we tend to feel what we imagine others feel. We love what we imagine others love, we hate what we imagine others hate and we desire what we imagine others desire (P31, P32). While this can lead to agreement and sympathy among people, it can easily lead to conflicts over things that everyone wants to possess (P32) and over the approval of others (P31S). Everyone is ambitious to be loved and praised by all and wants other people 'to live according to his temperament' (P31S). Given this fact, people inevitably end up hating and competing with one another.

The feelings of praise, blame, self-esteem, shame and repentance are heavily manipulated by human beings to make others behave in certain ways. Parents teach children to associate certain acts with praise or blame; throughout childhood and adolescence, social custom trains us to associate different acts with shame or esteem. The imaginary nature of such associations is demonstrated by the fact that different cultures assign praise and blame to different acts, as Spinoza explains in the Definitions of the Affects at the end of Part III: 'what among some is honourable, among others is dishonourable. Hence, according as each one has been educated, so he either repents of a deed or exults at being esteemed for it' (Def. Aff. XXVII). Three hundred years before the theories of Freud or Foucault, Spinoza argues that humans are *socially conditioned* to behave in certain ways because they have been trained to associate affects of joy with actions deemed 'right' and affects of sadness with actions deemed 'wrong'.

Being in Love

Spinoza mostly uses the term 'love' in a very general sense: it refers to love of friends, neighbours and family members, love of roses, music, money, chocolate, countries and football teams. Propositions 33–38, however, are about **passionate love** for another person, love that can easily become jealous and possessive. When we love another person, we strive to bring it about that he loves us in return; that is, that he feels joy accompanied by the idea of ourselves as cause (P33). And we feel more and more joy, and more and more esteemed, as we imagine that person to love us more; such is the exultation of being in love (P34). But if a lover betrays us, and we imagine that he 'is united with another by as close, or by a closer, bond of friendship than that with which [we ourselves], alone, possessed the thing, [we] will be affected with hate toward the thing [we] love, and will envy the other' (P35).

P35 and its scholium are among the most remarkable passages in the book. The proposition describes the jealousy that arises in imagining the person one loves in a sexual relationship with someone else. **Jealousy** is a complex feeling of vacillation between love and hatred for the person we love, combined with envy of their new lover. Moreover, Spinoza says, the hatred felt for one's former lover is greater depending on the amount of joy that person brought us in the past, and how we feel about the person they have left us for (P35S). If a lover leaves us for someone that we hate, our hatred will increase, because we will be forced to join the image of our former lover to the image of the thing we hate. Hating someone that we once loved is a stronger hatred than we feel for someone we have never loved (P38). Nevertheless, our desire to possess that person continues, and we desire to possess them in the same circumstances as when we first loved them (P36). But when we see that the circumstances of our joy are no longer present, we feel **longing** for the joy and love that are gone (P36S).

It is hard to imagine a more accurate description, in a philosophical text, of the powerful combination of emotions we experience in love and betrayal, and of the feelings that remain long after relationships have ended. Surely Spinoza writes from experience here, not from rational understanding. The explanation of jealousy needs no further elaboration, but Spinoza provides it anyway, giving us an example that can only come from personal experience of sexual jealousy:

He who imagines that a woman he loves prostitutes herself to another not only will be saddened, because his own appetite is restrained, but also will be repelled by her, because he is forced to join the image of the thing he loves to the shameful parts and excretions of the other. To this, finally, is added the fact that she no longer receives the jealous man with the same countenance as she used to offer him. From this cause, too, the lover is saddened. (P35S)

The strength of Spinoza's language here, the force of this example, leaves us in no doubt that he had direct experience of a sexual relationship that ended in betrayal. It indicates that Spinoza was powerfully affected by this encounter: he continues to feel saddened by the image of his lover joined to the 'shameful parts' of another man, and he longs for the time when his lover received him with joy. Here we have evidence that Spinoza, too, is a finite mode, powerfully affected by his experiences. No matter how rational a person becomes, he will never be able to avoid the affects altogether: they interrupt the flow of rational ideas and determine our thinking and acting. The rational thinking and writing of Part III has been interrupted in just this way for Spinoza in P35S.

Affects of Hatred and Anger

P39 tells us that we strive to do good to those we love and to do evil to those we hate, unless we fear that it will bring a greater evil to ourselves. **Fear** prevents us from doing things that love and hatred might otherwise cause us to do: we refuse to nurse a sick friend because we fear getting sick ourselves, or we stop ourselves from confronting a thug because we fear he will react violently.

In P39S, Spinoza reminds us (from P9S) that we call *good* that which we desire and *evil* that to which we are averse. Our desires and aversions are determined largely by our feelings. Since we desire joy and whatever leads to it, every kind of joy is good, and since we are averse to sadness and whatever leads to it, every kind of sadness is evil (P39S). This means that each person judges what is good and evil from his own affect: whatever makes him happy he will judge to be good, and whatever makes him unhappy he will judge to be evil. This leads to great disagreements among people as to what is good, best and most useful in life. But none of these people is *right* about what is good and what is bad because all these people are judging from their affects, that is, from those desires that are determined by the imagination. The greedy man *believes* an abundance of money is best, because money is what he most desires: but his desire for money comes from experience, not from his essence. We shall return to the question of good and evil in 'Part IV: Virtue, Ethics and Politics'.

Reciprocal hatred comes about as easily as reciprocal love. When we imagine that someone hates us unjustly, we hate that person in return, in the form of **anger** or **resentment** (P40). Naturally, we tend to think others' hatred for us is unjust, so 'it seldom happens' that we feel shame at imagining ourselves to be the cause of the hatred (P40S). Anger and resentment are much more common than shame. When we imagine that someone loves us without cause, we love them in return (in the sense of being positively disposed towards them). But when we imagine that someone we love hates us (P40C1), or that someone we hate loves us (P41C), we are torn by conflicting feelings of love and hatred.

We can see, then, that while hatred is increased by being returned, it can be diminished or destroyed by love (P43). If we imagine that a person we hate loves us, we may be moved to **cruelty** (P41S), but we will also start to imagine ourselves as the cause of that person's love and will strive to continue to please and bring joy to that person. The more love with which the hated person treats us, the more that love will efface our hatred; and when our hatred passes into love, our love is greater than if hatred had not preceded it (P44). It stands to reason: our joy, or *transition to greater perfection*, is greater if the transition has originated from a lower point of sadness than if it has originated from a neutral mid-point. The fact that hatred can be destroyed by love is the basis for accounts of **redemption**: the reformed criminal, the recovered drug addict, the misanthrope who learns to love life, all are people brought out of sadness, hatred and resentment by the love of others. The idea that love can conquer hatred plays an important role in Christian ethics (the irony of which Spinoza notes in his critique of religious repression and conflict in the *Theological-Political Treatise*, as quoted in the Introduction, above).

As we learned earlier, our love and hatred for things are often based on irrational factors such as their resemblance or contiguity to other things we love and hate. P46 gives us Spinoza's striking explanation of **ethnic hatred**, something that Spinoza, coming from a vilified minority community, must have had particular experience of. If someone has once been affected with sadness by someone of a different class or nation, and if he imagines that person as its cause 'under the universal name of the class or nation', then he will hate everyone of that class or nation (P46). By the same principle, people tend to love others on the basis of their nationality, race or class. These hatreds and loves are wholly irrational, for they are based on our imagining that individual people are determined by universal concepts of race, class or nationality. Such universal concepts are illegitimate, for they are simply imagined generalisations (IIP40S1). People are classified into races, classes and nations by virtue of linguistic conventions, not by virtue of their essence. For Spinoza, there is no rational basis for racism or nationalism, for loving the poor or hating the aristocracy. These feelings, like all the passive affects, are highly confused ideas which, unfortunately, are not easy to overcome.

Our love and hatred towards things are greater if we imagine those things to be free than if we imagine them to be necessary (P49). Things we imagine to be free are things we imagine to be the sole, free cause of their actions: we fixate our love or hatred on those things more than if we imagined other causes to be involved (P48). So, 'because men consider themselves to be free, they have a greater love or hate toward one another than toward other things' (P49S).

And because we consider *ourselves* free, our feelings of self-love and self-hatred (esteem and repentance) are particularly violent (P51S).

The fact that our bodies, experiences and associations change over time means that our own affects can change. Not only can an object affect different people in different ways, it can also affect the same person in different ways at different times (P51). People vary greatly in their affects – both in themselves and among one another. And because everyone judges what is good and bad from his own affect, 'it follows that men can vary as much in judgment as in affect' (P51S). Our judgements of others are based on our own affects and the affects we perceive them to feel. You may call someone a coward who fears something that, to you, is insignificant; he calls you foolhardy for not fearing something that to him is frightening. We may **admire** or **dread** someone because they seem to feel affects that are singular (P52) – imagining a leader's courage causes feelings of **wonder, veneration** and **devotion**, whereas dread at the imagined fury and vengeance of a dictator causes **consternation**.

External things are not the only causes of joy and sadness. We also feel these affects by reflecting on our own power. When the mind considers its power of thinking, it is necessarily *active*, and so we feel joy (P53), a joy that is encouraged as we imagine ourselves to be praised by others. But when the mind is restrained from considering its own power of thinking it is passive, and so we feel sadness (P55). This sadness at our lack of power is made worse if we imagine ourselves to be blamed by others. Joy and sadness that arise from considering our own power are **self-love** and **humility**. Since self-love arises whenever we consider our accomplishments, 'everyone is anxious to tell his own deeds, and show off his powers, both of body and of mind and . . . men, for this reason, are troublesome to one another' (P55S). Since everyone wants to affirm their own virtues and deny those of others, in order that they may be regarded as singularly worthy of praise, people are naturally envious of others' strengths and glad of others' weaknesses. 'It is clear, therefore, that men are naturally inclined to hate and envy' (P55S).

Because our essence is to strive to increase our power of thinking and acting, it is an essential part of what we are to feel this joy at our own power of thinking and acting, and it is quite natural that we seek to increase this joy through the praise of others. Our nature strives as hard as it can not to consider its own weakness, so that humility is rare (Def. Aff. XXIX). Indeed, Spinoza later suggests that humility is evidence of a diminished conatus. But it is easy to put on a show of humility – drawing attention to one's own weaknesses, praising the virtues of others, yielding to others' wishes, and so on – in order to gain the admiration of others. 'So those who are believed to be most despondent and humble are usually most ambitious and envious' (Def. Aff. XXIX), like the 'humble clerics' and 'humble servants' of the novels of Jane Austen and Charles Dickens.

The Particularity of the Affects

People are affected differently by different things. Our affects depend on the constitution of our particular bodies, on the experiences we have had and on the ways we associate images. This means that affects are radically particular: my love of coffee is different from anyone else's love of coffee, but furthermore, my love of *this* cup of coffee is different from my love of any other cup of coffee, because this affect of love is particular to *my body* in its encounter with *this cup of coffee*. And although I desire coffee every morning, each instance of that desire is different, because my body is subtly different on each occasion. (When I have a cold, my body is sufficiently changed that my desire for coffee is almost entirely diminished.) So, as Spinoza says in P56, there are as many species of joy, sadness, desire, love, hatred, etc., as there are species of object by which we are affected. And there are as many ways of feeling joy, sadness, etc. as there are individuals who feel them (P57). It is only by linguistic convention that we speak of 'love' or 'hatred' in general. The truth is that affects are specific to you and another specific object at a specific time: there are as many different affects as there are encounters (P56S).

Spinoza makes an interesting remark here about the feelings of animals. We know that animals have minds that are the ideas of their bodies, just as we do, and that animals are driven by their own conatus, just as we are. So animals feel desires to do that which is good for persevering in their being; they feel joy and sadness, the increase and decrease of their minds' and bodies' power or flourishing. Animal feelings are different from human feelings, because their essences differ from ours. As each being has a different essence, each one will feel different desires, joys and sadnesses and will be content with different things (P57S). The same applies to humans, who may be content with very different things in life: 'there is no small difference between the gladness by which a drunk is led and the gladness a philosopher possesses' (P57S).

The Active Affects

For much of Part III, Spinoza's concern has been with the passive affects: feelings that arise from our being *acted on* by external things and the association of images. The last two propositions of Part III depart from this analysis of the passive affects and speak instead of the *active* affects. At the outset of Part III, we learned that we are *active* when effects follow from our nature alone (D2) and that we *act* to the extent that our mind has adequate ideas (P1, P3).

Spinoza tells us in P58 that 'apart from the joy and desire which are passions, there are other affects of joy and desire which are related to us insofar as we act'. That is, there are some feelings of joy and desire which are *not related to imagination*, but instead arise with adequate ideas and our adequate causation of effects. When we have an adequate idea we know that we know it, and the mind necessarily considers its own power of thinking, leading to joy (P53). Furthermore, those desires through which we strive to persevere in our being do not come from experience or imagination, but from our very essence. As we are more active, our essence flourishes and those essential desires are intensified.

The joy and desire that are related to our activity are different from the joy and desire that arise from our passivity. There is a difference between the joy that we feel when we eat chocolate and the joy that we feel when we are the adequate cause of our actions. The former, passive joy relies on another thing, whereas the latter, active joy relies on ourselves alone. Similarly, the difference between the desire to please our parents and the desire to run away from danger is the difference between a desire that is determined by other people and a desire that is determined by our essence. Passive joys are important in increasing our power to act and think, just as imagination is important in increasing our rational knowledge: the joy we gain in experience contributes to our ability to gain adequate ideas and to feel active joy in our increased power.

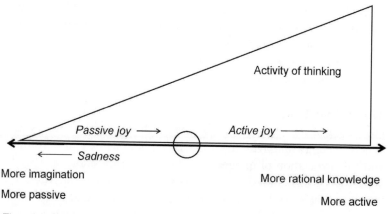

Figure 3.1 Conatus, activity and knowledge

Is there also an 'active sadness'? P59 tells us that 'active sadness' is impossible because it is a contradictory concept. Sadness necessarily involves the diminishment of the mind and body's power to act; it cannot arise from activity, but is necessarily associated with passivity. Insofar as we are saddened, we are necessarily passive. Thus all our sadness is determined by external things; sadness cannot come from our essence, and we cannot feel sadness insofar as we are the full, adequate cause of our actions. Affects of sadness, like inadequate ideas, indicate that we are finite modes who necessarily interact with other things. But perhaps we can overcome the sad passions if we can become more active and have more adequate ideas – if we become more rational.

Figure 3.1 shows how the joy–sadness continuum maps onto the imagination–reason continuum represented in Figure 2.4. As we imagine more, we are more passive to external things and we feel more sadness and passive joy. But as we understand more and gain more adequate ideas, we are more active, which involves more active joy. The circle on the joy–sadness line is the conatus of the finite mode, which increases in size as it moves right, towards greater activity, and decreases in size as it moves left, towards lesser activity. Conatus strives to move towards the right, increasing in power and activity and gaining more and more active joy.

The relationship between reason and the affects will be discussed further in 'Part IV: Virtue, Ethics and Politics'. For now, it is time to close the present section with Spinoza's most enduring metaphor: 'From what has been said it is clear that we are driven about in many ways by external causes, and that, like waves on the sea, driven by contrary winds, we toss about, not knowing our outcome and our fate' (P59S). A finite mode is a wave on the sea: it rises from the infinite continuum of being, it is pushed and pulled by contrary forces, not knowing its direction or the bigger currents that cause its movement, and eventually destroyed by another wave, it disintegrates, back into the sea from which it came. Given that this is what it means to be a finite mode, how should we live our lives? This will be explored next.

Part III ends with two helpful summaries: the Definitions of the Affects and the General Definition of the Affects.

Part IV: Virtue, Ethics and Politics

Part IV of the *Ethics* is where Spinoza sets out his ethics: his theory of how to live well. In this section we look at Spinoza's idea of virtue and his understanding of good and evil, then consider the recommendations for ethical behaviour and political organisation that follow from it.

The material in this section raises a lot of questions. Can Spinoza's definitions of good and bad be made consistent with moral action? Does Spinoza's denial of intentions and free will mean that he denies moral responsibility? If all value judgements are subjective, can there be an objective ethics? Ultimately, can we live our lives according to Spinoza's ethical programme? In helping you to read Part IV, the aim of this section is to give you the resources to address these questions and to consider critically ethical problems from a Spinozist standpoint.

Spinoza's views on ethics may well challenge your own beliefs, or, like Nietzsche, you may find that Spinoza expresses something that you have long believed to be right. Either way, you will find Spinoza's ethics surprising, both in its denial of universal moral values and in its affirmation of rational knowledge as the key to living and acting well. At the very least, Part IV will give you a new way to think about ethical and political issues.

Enslavement

In Part III we learned that our behaviour and actions are determined by passive affects of joy, sadness and desire, affects that arise in experience and are connected to our *images* of things. We are constantly pushed and pulled by *feelings based on images*: we strive to fulfil what we imagine we desire, to benefit those we imagine bring us joy and to harm those we imagine bring us sadness. Under these conditions, human beings are driven by love, hatred, ambition, pride, resentment, envy and other passions that bring them into conflict with one another. Since we are part of nature, constantly encountering other things, we are necessarily subject to the affects and necessarily the inadequate cause of our actions.

Jump ahead briefly to the first few propositions of Part IV. Spinoza makes it clear here that it is impossible that we should stand apart from nature, undergoing only those changes that come about through our nature alone (P4). In other words, since we are necessarily interconnected with the things we use and rely on, it is impossible for us to be unaffected by them and to be the adequate cause of all our actions. If a human being could be entirely unaffected by other things, he would never perish. But 'the force by which a man perseveres in existing is limited, and infinitely surpassed by the power of external causes' (P3). We cannot survive and flourish forever, because there are always things in nature more powerful than ourselves that can destroy us (A1).

Spinoza sees our subjection to the affects as a kind of enslavement, which explains the title of Part IV: 'Of Human Bondage, or the Powers of the Affects'. Bondage is 'man's lack of power to moderate and restrain the affects' (IV Pref.). You may think it strange to use the terminology of enslavement to describe our inability to control our feelings. But bondage suggests that something has been deprived of the power to determine itself, and when we are passive to the affects, that is precisely our predicament: we are less able to cause effects through our own nature. 'The man who is subject to affects is under the control, not of himself, but of fortune, in whose power he so greatly is that often, though he sees the better for himself, he is still forced to follow the worse' (IV Pref.).

Spinoza aims to demonstrate that enslavement to the affects causes people to do things that are bad for them – that is, things that are bad for their survival and well-being. Enslavement to a desire for nicotine, for instance, leads a person to smoke cigarettes which diminish his life. But enslavement to the affects is often more complex. Love can lead a person to remain in an abusive relationship that is bad for her flourishing. Ambition, resentment, hatred and envy lead neighbours into conflict and nations into war. From fear, people may support a ruler who deprives them of their power to act and think. In these ways, enslavement to the affects leads readily to forms of social and political enslavement. People who are powerfully affected by sadness, hatred, anger and fear are easily influenced and manipulated by other forces: they are highly vulnerable to gangs, religious cults and extreme political parties, for instance.

Good and Evil

How does Spinoza know that our determination by the affects causes us to do things that are *bad* for us? How does he understand good and bad, such that he is able to make this claim? We know that Spinoza rejects absolute moral values. In the Appendix to Part I, he argued that value terms such as 'good, evil, order, confusion, beauty, ugliness' are based on what is useful to human beings. Nothing in nature is *in itself* good or evil, because everything in nature is a mode of God. From God's perspective, things are neither good nor evil; they simply are what they are. Finite modes, however, judge things to be good or evil because they are good or evil *to them*. Each individual judges something to be good because he likes and desires it, or evil because he hates and avoids it (I App., IIIP9S). In the Preface to Part IV, Spinoza reiterates this point:

As far as good and evil are concerned, they indicate nothing positive in things, considered in themselves, nor are they anything other than modes of thinking, or notions we form because we compare things to one another. For one and the same thing can, at the same time, be good, and bad, and also indifferent. For example, music is good for one who is melancholy, bad for one who is mourning, and neither good nor bad to one who is deaf.

Good and bad are not objective values that can be assigned to things, but vary according to the desires and affects of the judging individual. So Spinoza defines good and evil in D1 and D2: 'By good I shall understand what we certainly know to be useful to us. By evil, however, I shall understand what we certainly know prevents us from being masters of some good.'

On the face of it, these definitions look gravely problematic. Is Spinoza really saying that moral values are entirely subjective, that anything useful to us is *good* and that anything preventing our attainment of something useful is *evil*? The execution of Anne Boleyn was useful to Henry VIII, but surely it wasn't morally good. Displacing a fishing community to build a hotel seems good to the property developers, evil to the fishermen: is there no objective truth about the morality of this situation that we can appeal to? It looks as if Spinoza's relativism about moral values can valorise any action on the basis of its subjective utility.

When we look at D1 and D2 more carefully, we see that this objection loses its force. Spinoza says: 'by good I shall understand what we *certainly know* to be useful to us'. Remember that to *certainly know* something is very different from merely believing it. Beliefs are inadequate knowledge: they are necessarily uncertain and involve falsity and error (see the section on adequate and inadequate knowledge in Part II above). To have certain knowledge is to have an adequate idea, to understand some aspect of your nature fully and truly, through reason. When we certainly know something to be useful to us, we truly understand that some external thing or action is useful for our nature – we *know* that it increases our life's flourishing. And when we certainly know that something prevents us from mastering some good, we truly understand that some external thing or action decreases our life's flourishing.

Since what we strive for to enhance our flourishing varies according to circumstances, the same thing can be good, bad or indifferent, as music is in Spinoza's example. This tells us that, for Spinoza, values can be neither universal nor transcendent. 'Good' and 'evil' mean what is good and bad for *this individual's flourishing at this time*. These values do not apply universally to all individuals and are not imposed on the individual from any external source; they are immanent to the nature of the individual. Since we have the potential for full, true understanding of our nature, we have the potential to understand what is truly good and evil for us at any given time.

However, this potential is never fully realised. Most of the time, because we lack adequate knowledge of our own nature, we are uncertain of what is good and evil for our flourishing. Instead, we make judgements about good and evil based on our associations of images with affects. Inevitably, those judgements are inadequate and are frequently erroneous, so in doing what we believe to be good, we often do things that are truly evil. Henry VIII may have believed that it was good to execute his wife, but his belief was false, based on anger and imagined betrayal. If he had truly understood his own nature, he would have known that killing another person was bad for his own flourishing. (We shall understand the reasons for this later in Part IV.)

Given this view of good and evil, how should we understand Spinoza's remarks in the Preface that we should form and follow 'a model of human nature', and that 'good' and 'evil' refer to our proximity or distance from such a moral model? Moral models are useful because we do not always know what is truly good and evil for us. Since we lack complete understanding of our essence, it is best for us to follow a model of good action, based on the rational understanding we are able to accrue. We must gain as much rational understanding as we can of our nature and what is good for it, which is one of the purposes of Part IV.

Spinoza rejects the notion that good and evil are absolute values that apply to things 'objectively'. From the perspective of God or nature, nothing is either good or evil, just as nothing is beautiful or ugly, ordered or disordered. God does not demand good or condemn evil, for God does not make judgements or plans. Moral values are not imposed by God; they exist from the perspective of the modes alone. In that sense, Spinoza is a relativist about values. But it is not the case that Spinoza takes values to be arbitrary, subjective inventions without any foundation in truth. Certainly, when they are based on images, affects, traditions and habit, 'good' and 'evil' are fictional constructs. But when they are immanent to the individual's essence, 'good' and 'evil' are real and true. For each individual, there are things that are truly good which promote its being, and things that are truly evil which detract from it.

Virtue
We are now in a position to understand Spinoza's concept of virtue. Bypass the other definitions and look at D8:

By virtue and power I understand the same thing, that is, virtue, insofar as it is related to man, is the very essence, or nature, of man, insofar as he has the power of bringing about certain things, which can be understood through the laws of his nature alone.

This definition links virtue to the notions of activity and adequate causation which we discussed in 'Part III: The Affects'. We know that the essence of a thing is its conatus, its striving to persevere in its being (IIIP7). When we are determined to act by our essence, we are the adequate cause of effects: we are caused to act by our nature alone and we do those things that follow from our own nature. Those things necessarily promote our survival and flourishing (IIIP9S). In other words, when we are active, our activity is determined by our essence and we necessarily do what is good for us. When we do what is good for us, our essence flourishes and our power to act increases. This, for Spinoza, is *virtue*: our power to act according to our nature alone.

Virtue, therefore, is not a tag that we bestow on people for acts deemed to have moral worth. Virtue is the *power* of each individual to *actualise its essence*. Every individual has this power, but, as we have seen, the power of an individual waxes and wanes as it is affected by external forces. This means that every individual has virtue, but our virtue increases or decreases as our activity increases or decreases. A person is more virtuous as she is increasingly capable of being the adequate cause of those things that follow from her nature. She does more things that are good for her, increasing her virtue still more. But a person is less virtuous as this capability decreases. The person who is more acted on by external things, and is only the partial or inadequate cause of her actions, is less active, less powerful and less virtuous. She does things that are bad for her, because she is less capable of doing what her own nature determines her to do and she will be increasingly determined by external forces.

As a person is more passive to the affects, then, his virtue decreases. Those who suffer from powerful affects are on a downward spiral: affects of sadness and pain decrease their flourishing and virtue, making them even more liable to affects, more open to external influence and less likely to do what is good for them. So long as we are enslaved to the affects, we remain passive to determination by other things, with little power and little virtue. But if we can find a way to become less enslaved to the affects, to become less passive and more active, then we will have discovered a way to increase our virtue. That is an upward spiral: as we are less affected by things, we are more able to act from our nature and do what is good for us. Living virtuously, then, depends on freeing ourselves from enslavement to the affects.

The Power of the Affects

This project requires us to understand the power the affects have over us, for 'man is necessarily always subject to passions' (P4C). This is the purpose of P5–18. A human being is a mode of power that waxes and wanes according to the force of the other powers around him. Since the passions are caused in part by external things, their force is defined by the power of an external cause (P5); and since, due to A1, that power can far surpass our own, the force of any passion can overcome our power and activity. No matter how active a person becomes, they may still be overpowered by an affect that 'stubbornly clings' to them (P6).

So, can these powerful affects be restrained? Yes, Spinoza says, but only by 'an affect opposite to, and stronger than, the affect to be restrained' (P7). The reason for this is that affects involve changes of the body as well as feelings of the mind. A bodily change can only be displaced by another, more forceful bodily change. When the body changes, the mind's feeling changes too. In everyday terms, very powerful emotions cannot be quickly removed unless other, more powerful emotions of the same nature force them out: your sadness at your football team losing will immediately be overcome by your sadness at failing an exam (or vice versa, depending on which sadness, for you, is the more powerful).

The power of an affect also varies depending on whether we imagine its cause to be present, future or past (P9, P10) and on whether we imagine it to be necessary, contingent or possible (P11, P12, P13). The intensity of the affects is tied to the intensity of the images connected to them: as things are more present to mind, we are more strongly affected by them; and as their presence fades, the affects fade too. Similarly, we are more powerfully affected by things we imagine to be necessary than by things we imagine to be contingent (existing things whose necessity is unclear to us, D3) or merely possible (non-existing things whose necessity is unclear to us, D4).

But things we imagine to be contingent or possible can be more powerful, depending on whether we imagine them to be present or future (P12C): our present worries tend to affect us more strongly than the prospect of death, which is necessary but far in the future.

In P14–17, Spinoza shows that passive affects are so powerful that they can overcome even those *active desires* determined by our essence alone and the *active joy* we feel as our activity increases (see IIIP58). Our essence determines us to desire what is truly good for us and to avoid what is truly evil for us. To the extent that we are conscious of these essential desires, we have true knowledge of good and evil (see P8) and we act from our own power. But these desires can be 'extinguished or restrained' by passive desires and affects, because the power of external things can far exceed our own power (P15). This means that our *essential* desires for what *truly* enhances our flourishing are often overpowered by desires determined by external things – desires for 'the pleasures of the moment' (P16). We are frequently determined to do what we *imagine* will bring us joy, even when we *know* that another course of action would be better (P17S). Because desires arising from joy are stronger than desires arising from sadness (P18), it is passive joy that leads us astray, causing us to pursue imaginary goods rather than true ones.

Spinoza's point that imagination can overpower true knowledge may seem to be at odds with his general view that true knowledge corrects the errors of imagination. But he is clear that when we come to understand something rationally, 'the error is removed, not the imagination' (P1S). Our bodily experience of the sun suggests it is about 200 feet away; when we come to understand the true distance of the sun from the earth, this erroneous belief is removed, but since our bodies continue to be affected by the sun in the same way, our *imagination* of the sun is unchanged (P1S, IIP35S). Similarly, when a smoker comes to understand that cigarettes are bad for his health, his erroneous belief in their goodness will be removed, but his imagination of them, and the affects of desire and joy he associates with them, will remain. External things continue to have a pull on us even when we know they are not good for us. True knowledge as such has no power to overcome these affects; only insofar as that true knowledge is *felt* as an essential desire that is more powerful than other affects will it be able to overcome them (P14).

Seeking our own Advantage

In the scholium to P18 Spinoza remarks that he has explained 'the causes of men's lack of power and inconstancy, and why men do not observe the precepts of reason'. Quite simply, people do not observe the precepts of reason because they are powerfully affected and determined by images and feelings. Spinoza gives a preliminary sketch of these precepts here, which are the basis of his ethics and which will be explained in the remainder of Part IV. Briefly, they are:

- Virtue is based on each person striving to preserve his being.
- Virtue is desirable for its own sake, not for the sake of any other end.
- Suicide cannot be virtuous.
- It is virtuous to join together with other people.
- People who are virtuous want what is best both for themselves and for others.

Spinoza sets these principles out here, prior to demonstrating them, because he knows that his central idea is controversial: that striving for self-preservation is the foundation of virtue. He wants to assure readers in advance that this principle leads not to immorality and selfishness, as might first appear, but rather to virtue, morality and cooperation.

We have seen that each person's nature determines him to want what is good for him and to avoid what is evil for him (P19). Here is another way of putting this: in striving to persevere in our being, we are determined to seek what is most useful or advantageous to us. Our nature determines us to seek our own advantage, and when we act according to the laws of our nature alone, we do exactly that. This means that virtue – our power to act according to the laws of our nature alone – lies in seeking our own advantage. P20 is the central tenet of Spinoza's ethical system:

The more each one strives, and is able, to seek his own advantage, that is, to preserve his being, the more he is endowed with virtue; conversely, insofar as each one neglects his own advantage, that is, neglects to preserve his being, he lacks power.

Spinoza's demonstration is straightforward. Virtue is our power to strive to persevere in our being. The more each person strives and is able to flourish, the more virtue he has. The person who neglects his own advantage and fails to preserve his being and to flourish lacks power and therefore virtue.

Spinoza makes some striking remarks here about suicide. In P18S he says that 'those who kill themselves are weak-minded and completely conquered by external causes contrary to their nature'. This idea is expanded in P20S. Since every individual's essence is the striving to preserve their being, it cannot be that anyone's essence could determine them to *neglect* to preserve their being. An individual cannot destroy itself from its own essence: death and destruction necessarily come about through external causes (IIIP4). A person who seeks to destroy his own being, then, does not act from his essence at all: he is completely overcome and 'defeated' by external forces contrary to his nature. External powers literally force his hand, as in the examples in P20S. Suicide, for Spinoza, is not an act of self-determination, but its opposite. The person who commits suicide is so overpowered by affects of despair that he ceases to strive to preserve himself. Such a person is unfortunate indeed, for he is so much enslaved to the affects that he has become entirely passive to them and his essence ceases its striving activity altogether. This person is *weak* in both body and mind: he is at the lowest degree of power and activity in every respect.

Move now to P22C: 'the striving to preserve oneself is the first and only foundation of virtue. For no other principle can be conceived prior to this one, and no virtue can be conceived without it.' The *desire to be* is the most basic desire there is. It is our essence; no other virtue can be conceived without it (P21). We are modes of God's power of being, actualising that being in a certain and determinate way, and this, our essence, must be the basis of our ethics.

Virtue and Reason

In the next six propositions we learn how virtue is linked to reason: insofar as we have more rational understanding, we are more virtuous. The connection is explained in P23. Insofar as someone is determined to act by inadequate ideas, he is the inadequate cause of what he does; his actions do not follow from his nature alone and they lack virtue. When we understand rationally, we have adequate ideas and we are the adequate cause of our actions. Being the adequate cause

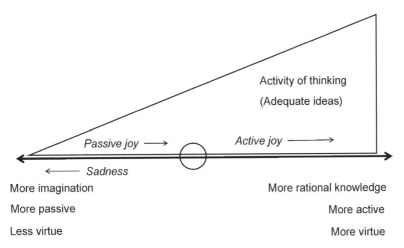

Figure 4.1 Virtue and reason

of our actions is acting from our nature alone. So we act from virtue only insofar as we have adequate ideas (P23).

We are now ready to revise Figure 3.1. Figure 4.1 shows that as the individual increases his activity of thinking (i.e. gains more adequate ideas) he becomes more active (i.e. the adequate cause of his actions), increasing both his rational knowledge and his virtue. We can see too that joy – especially active joy – is linked to increasing virtue. As in Figure 3.1, the circle is the individual's conatus, which shrinks as it moves down the scale and expands as it moves up the scale.

In seeking our own advantage, we seek what preserves our being and brings us joy, particularly the active joy that is involved with being the adequate cause of our actions. To seek our own advantage is to seek life, activity and virtue. Virtue is necessarily tied to reason. Acting from virtue, therefore, is 'acting, living, and preserving our being (these three signify the same thing) by the guidance of reason, from the foundation of seeking one's own advantage' (P24).

Insofar as we think rationally, our minds strive for understanding. This is because the essence of our mind *is* true understanding and its striving is to persevere and increase its being (P26). Virtue involves not only rational knowledge, but the ongoing striving for more rational knowledge. (As with all things in Spinoza's universe, virtue is not a static state, but an ongoing activity.) Insofar as we think rationally, we truly understand something about our own nature: that we want and need more true understanding. In other words, we *certainly know* that what leads to true understanding is good for us and that what impedes true understanding is evil (P27).

We have learned that the foundation of ethics is seeking our own advantage. And now we have our first ethical principle: that which leads to true understanding is truly good and that which impedes true understanding is truly evil. It follows that the mind's greatest good is to have as much true understanding as possible; that is, true understanding of infinite being, or God (P28). Our greatest virtue, then, is to 'know God' – not in a religious sense, but in the sense of gaining as much true knowledge as we can about reality. The path to virtue involves increasing our understanding of ourselves and our world through empirical encounters that build common notions and rational understanding.

Ethics and other People: the Rational Community

The next set of propositions, P29–36, is a template for how we can build true understanding and virtue through cooperation with other individuals. It sets out an ethics of interpersonal relations that builds up to Spinoza's theory of politics in P37.

In Part II we looked at *common notions* as the building blocks of rational knowledge (you may wish to re-read that section now). The doctrine of common notions silently underlies this section of Part IV, where Spinoza argues that in order to maximise our rational knowledge, we must combine forces with beings whose nature is similar to our own. The reason for this is simple: when we interact with beings of a similar nature, we are in the best position to clarify those common notions that are immanent to our own nature and to the nature of those other beings. In other words, interacting with other human beings is the surest way to build adequate ideas and rational knowledge, and therefore virtue.

P29 tells us that nothing can be either good or evil for us unless it has something in common with our nature. That is because a thing whose nature is entirely different from ours cannot interact with us at all and therefore cannot aid or restrain our power of acting. But there is nothing in our world that has *nothing* in common with us: all physical bodies agree in certain things, namely their existence in the attribute of extension and their motion and rest (IIL2). So P29 is telling us, in an oblique way, that everything in the attributes of thinking and extension can be good or evil for us, and therefore that everything in our world is morally relevant to us. The only things that are *not* morally relevant are things that exist in other attributes – things that we can never experience or know in any case.[3]

Now, nothing can be evil for us through what it has in common with our nature because if it were, that commonality that is part of our nature would itself be evil for us (P30). What is in our nature is necessarily good for us, so, to the extent that other things share aspects of our nature, they must be good for us (P31). This means that 'the more a thing agrees with our nature, the more useful, or better, it is for us' (P31C). Other human beings, who share the same basic bodily composition and have the same basic capacities for acting and feeling, are good for us. Through interacting with others, we gain adequate ideas of our common natures, compositions and capacities, thereby increasing our knowledge and activity.

Not all human beings are equally good for us. Insofar as people are subject to the passions, they do not agree in nature, for they are determined differently by different external forces, and their different feelings mean that they frequently come into conflict (P32, P33, P34). When people are subject to the passions, they differ in nature and are contrary to one another: strongly affected, irrational people are not good for us and indeed can be evil for us (P30). We should either avoid such people, or – better – help them to restrain their affects and become more rational.

When people live according to the guidance of reason, they agree in nature and then they are good for one another (P35). Let us look

---

[3] Spinoza's remark that stones and men 'agree in nothing' (P32S) seems to contradict this. But this remark is intended to illustrate that negation cannot be the basis of agreement. While certainly it would be absurd to say that stones and humans 'agree' by virtue of their inability to fly (for instance), Spinoza cannot mean that stones and humans do not have *anything* in common. For he cannot deny that stones and humans agree in extension and motion and rest. Furthermore, stones can be good for us (in building houses) and evil for us (in a fatal rock-slide). Since they are morally relevant to us, it must be that their nature is not *entirely* different from ours.

at Spinoza's demonstration for this point. Insofar as people have rational knowledge, they act more from their own nature. In these cases, reason truly understands those things that follow from human nature and it truly understands what is good for human nature. And so, insofar as people live according to the guidance of reason, they do what is truly good not only for themselves, but for human nature too (P35Dem.).

But there is a problem here. Spinoza can justifiably claim that insofar as people are rational, they do what is good for their own *particular* natures. But in P35 he claims that insofar as people are rational, they do what is good for *human nature* in general. There seems to be a hidden assumption at work here: that each person's particular nature is actually a species of some general 'human nature'. Where did this idea of 'human nature' come from and how can Spinoza justify it, given his distrust of universal terms and universal values?

To solve this problem we need to think about what it means for individuals to have common natures. Look back at Figure 2.2: each individual body (D) is the expression of certain relations of motion and rest (C). Those relations of motion and rest are specifically constitutive of the individual body. But many elements of that constitutive relation are *generic* and common to multiple bodies. For example, your body has the ability of self-propulsion, based on a certain relation of motion and rest that is common to all mammals. The relation of motion and rest that determines self-propulsion is then progressively specified according to further relations of motion and rest: relations that are specific to mammals that move on land, relations that are specific to mammals that can move on two legs, relations that are specific to humans, and relations that are specific to *this* human. So the bodily nature of each individual is specific to it, but each individual also shares a great deal of its nature with other individuals. We share most with other humans, less with primates, less still with other mammals, and so on.

This is how we must understand Spinoza's reference to 'human nature'. Each human being has its own specific bodily nature, but a great deal of that nature is held in common with other human beings, who are constitutively very similar. This means that there *is* a common 'human nature', defined not through imaginary universals or philosophers' definitions, but through *what our bodies have in common*. When people have more rational knowledge, they have a better understanding of the nature of their own bodies and a better understanding of the nature of human bodies generally. And so, when people have more rational knowledge, they understand not only what is good for them as individuals, but also what is good for human beings generally.

This means that there is nothing in nature that is better for us than a person who lives according to the guidance of reason (P35C1). This person agrees best with our nature and is good for us. She is good for us in the sense that in doing what is good for her own nature, she does what is good for human nature too. This is the import of P35C2: 'When each man most seeks his own advantage for himself, then men are most useful to one another.' Spinoza's extremely clear explanation sums up his ethical position:

> For the more each one seeks his own advantage, and strives to preserve himself, the more he is endowed with virtue, or what is the same, the greater is his power of acting according to the laws of his own nature, that is, of living from the guidance of reason. But men most agree in nature, when they live according to the guidance of reason. Therefore, men will be most useful to one another, when each one most seeks his own advantage. (P35C2Dem.)

Any notion that Spinoza's ethics is selfish is put to rest by this corollary. Seeking our own advantage is not a matter of doing what is in our own personal interest at the expense of others. If we act selfishly, then we are doing merely what we *believe* to be advantageous to us. But if we *truly* seek our own advantage, we act from true understanding of what is good, both for ourselves and for others. To be sure, seeking our own advantage is acting in our own self-interest, but importantly, it means acting in the interests of every other human being as well. The person who *most* seeks his own advantage – who has the clearest understanding of what is good for human nature and acts on it – is *best* for other people.

Of course, it rarely happens that people live according to the guidance of reason, as Spinoza acknowledges in P35S. Because they are more often guided by their affects, people typically do not seek what is truly to their own or humanity's advantage. But despite people's irrationality, disagreements and conflicts, it is better for them to join forces and help one another than to live a solitary life. We preserve our own being most effectively when we work together; a person living entirely outside of human society is unlikely to survive for long. 'To man, there is nothing more useful than man' (P18S).

Furthermore, two individuals of the same nature joined together 'compose an individual twice as powerful as each one' (P18S). In 'Part II: Minds, Bodies, Experience and Knowledge', we saw that a human being is one individual, but a group of people communicating their motion to one another and moving as one is a bigger individual. Now we see just how important that idea is. A group of human beings working together – a *community* – is more powerful and capable than any number of disconnected individuals. A community has more physical capabilities and therefore more mental capabilities too. By joining with others with whom we have a lot in common, we increase our adequate ideas, making the whole community increasingly capable of thinking and acting. The best community is composed of rational people who *together* build their understanding of the world. It is to every individual's advantage to build a rational community, for it is there that we are most likely to gain understanding and virtue.

Man, I say, can wish for nothing more helpful to the preservation of his being than that all should so agree in all things that the minds and bodies of all would compose, as it were, one mind and one body; that all should strive together, as far as they can, to preserve their being; and that all, together, should seek for themselves the common advantage of all. (P18S)

This tells us something important about how we should treat other human beings. It can never be good to harm another human being, because in doing so we reduce the power of something that is truly useful to us and diminish the prospects of building a rational community. It is impossible that our nature should determine us to harm another person, for then we would act contrary to our own advantage. Anyone who imagines that it is to his advantage to harm someone else is neither rational nor virtuous. The virtuous person strives never to harm or destroy another person, but to preserve him, and to help him to become more rational and virtuous too.

This is the import of P37: the good that the virtuous person wants for himself, he also wants for others. The virtuous person knows that rational knowledge is truly good for him and for human nature. Since rational people are good for us, we naturally strive both that we should be rational and that other people should be rational too. It is good to strive to increase the understanding of oneself and others – through teaching and listening, reading and writing books, and engaging in the exchange of ideas. The person who can foster rationality in herself and in others has a high degree of virtue and power (P37S1). Spinoza must have seen himself as this kind of rational teacher.

However, a person who strives to make others live according to what he imagines to be good, based on his affects, is hateful to others. Alas, when people strive that others should love what they love and live according to their temperament, they inevitably come into conflict, because these imaginary goods – money, fame, objects of desire – cannot easily be shared. With this, Spinoza says that he has shown the difference between true and imaginary virtue:

> True virtue is nothing but living according to the guidance of reason, and so lack of power consists only in this, that a man allows himself to be guided by things outside him, and to be determined by them to do what the common constitution of external things demands, not what his own nature, considered in itself, demands. (P37S1)

The truly virtuous person has greater rational knowledge of, and acts according to, her own nature. The virtuous person is *powerful* because she is more active, both mentally and physically: she has adequate knowledge of more of her nature and is the adequate cause of more of her actions. She does what is truly good both for herself and for others and strives to increase the rationality, virtue and activity of all of humanity.

The non-virtuous person has a mind taken up by images and affects, and acts according to the impulses and demands of external things. He lacks power because he is less active: he has inadequate knowledge of much of his nature and is the inadequate cause of most of his actions. He does what he imagines is good for himself, but these activities are often truly bad for him and for others. He frequently finds himself in conflict with others, particularly over the possession of external things, and will often be at odds with his community.

The bad person is not morally bad: rather, he is bad at being a person. He is bad at recognising, understanding and actualising his own essence. The good person is good at being a person. But no one is wholly good or wholly bad. We cannot be 100% rational and virtuous, because we are necessarily subject to affects (P4). Similarly, we cannot be 100% irrational and non-virtuous, because we necessarily have some adequate ideas (IIP38). Every one of us is to some extent good, to some extent bad. But this proportion is not fixed: our virtue and activity can take a nose-dive when we are suddenly confronted with devastating news or it can increase through the guidance of a rational teacher. We move up and down the scale of virtue and activity as we gain rational understanding and are affected by our experiences.

Ethics and Animals

The first scholium to P37 ends with Spinoza's ethical position on animals. Unlike every other philosopher of his time, Spinoza does not claim that humans are superior to animals by virtue of reason. For Spinoza, non-human animals are capable of becoming more rational and active, and of increasing their power by forming groups. Animals will achieve less rational understanding and activity than humans, because their minds and bodies are less complex (IIP13S). Their virtue and affects are different from ours, for different things are good for their natures (IIP57S). But there is no difference in kind between humans and other animals: we are all finite modes striving to preserve our being.

This fact pitches creatures against each another. All animals seek to make use of others to ensure their survival and to destroy those that pose a threat to them. Humans therefore have a natural 'right' to kill and make use of animals in any way that is advantageous to them, just as wolves and sharks do. Spinoza accepts that animals have sensations, but argues that we may 'consider our own advantage, use them at our pleasure, and treat them as is most convenient for us. For they do not agree in nature with us, and their affects are different in nature from human affects' (P37S1). Since we cannot form a rational community with anything non-human, reason does not demand that we preserve it, but determines us to 'adapt it to our use in any way whatever' (IV App. XXVI).

Readers are often struck by an apparent discrepancy here. On the one hand, Spinoza claims that animals are not radically different from humans. But on the other, he seems to deny that we have any moral responsibility towards them. How should we understand Spinoza's ethical position on animals?

First, Spinoza's claim that animals 'do not agree in nature with us' does not mean that animals have *nothing* in common with us. We share a certain amount of our nature, more with some animals than others (see my explanations of P29 and P35, above). Not only are some animals (such as chimpanzees) compositionally very similar to us; humans work with animals to compose bigger, more powerful individuals (as in the case of a blind person with a guide dog). We have more in common with chimpanzees and dogs than we do with sea-slugs and mosquitoes. It is no coincidence, then, that we worry more about the ethics of using primates in scientific experiments than about the ethics of killing insects. For Spinoza, animals *are* morally relevant to us, to varying degrees – not by virtue of any intrinsic moral status, but by virtue of their compositional similarity to us and their capacity to help us compose more powerful communities.

Second, we must consider animals' ethical status in terms of the principle of seeking our own advantage. We use rivers to draw water, kill chickens for food and employ dogs to guard our property. Those activities have ethical merit, for Spinoza, since they contribute to our flourishing. But those activities cease to have ethical merit when they detract from our flourishing. If we pollute rivers, overcrowd chickens and mistreat dogs, our water will be contaminated, our food will poison us, and our community will be open to attack. It is in our interest, and the interest of building the rational community, to treat animals and natural resources in a sustainable way which allows us to continue to make use of them for our own flourishing.

Factory farming offers a nice case study for Spinoza's ethics. For Spinoza, it is ethically good to eat meat: no other food is as beneficial for our survival. It is ethically good, too, to farm animals in a way that gives more and more people the opportunity to eat meat, increasing the survival and flourishing of human individuals who contribute to bigger and stronger communities. But it is ethically bad to farm animals so intensively that they are malformed and disease-ridden, producing poor quality meat of low nutritional benefit. It is bad because it is bad for human flourishing, not because it is bad for the animals.

This is the key to solving ethical problems from a Spinozist standpoint: working together, we must strive for rational understanding of what is *truly* in the interests of human nature and base our actions solely on that. In many cases, we do not yet know what is truly best for human nature. In the case of factory farming, the human community has not yet come to understand whether it is truly better to give chickens better living conditions or to give poorer people greater access to meat. But on Spinoza's view, anyone who approaches the problem from the perspective of animals' moral rights, or out of sentiment for animals' feelings, is seriously misguided. He is saying that our attitude to animals must be guided by rational understanding of what is truly to our advantage, not by imagining what is to the animals' advantage or by pity for what animals may feel.

Politics, Laws and the State

Let us move now to the second scholium of P37, where Spinoza discusses politics. In common with other early modern political philosophers (notably Thomas Hobbes), Spinoza presents the civil state as a solution to the ills of the 'state of nature'. In *Leviathan* (1651), Hobbes imagines human life prior to the development of the civil state. He concludes that in this 'state of nature', each person had an equal right to seek his own advantage and was in constant conflict with others over resources, with the result that human life was 'poor, nasty, brutish and short' (Hobbes 1968: 186). To escape this situation, it was necessary for people to give their right over to a sovereign who prevented conflict through a system of laws, threats and incentives: the basis of the civil state.

Spinoza was strongly influenced by Hobbes, but with an important difference. Like Hobbes, Spinoza believes that people are driven by seeking their own advantage. But unlike Hobbes, he believes that there are good and bad ways of doing this. In a world where everyone was completely determined by their passions, each person would seek what they *imagined* to be to their advantage, leading to constant conflict. In this 'state of nature', each person would judge what was good and bad, just and unjust, according to his own affects, and would do whatever he irrationally desired. For Spinoza as for Hobbes, this would be a state of fear, hatred, violence and anarchy.

But picture a world in which every person is fully rational and fully virtuous, a world in which nobody is determined by their passions and in which everybody does what is best for humankind. In this world, everyone will seek their own advantage, but they will do so in a way that is necessarily good both for themselves and for others. In this perfect rational community, no laws will be required, for each person will follow his own nature without any injury to others (P37S2). People will exist in perfect harmony, doing only those things that accord with their own nature and with the nature of everyone else.

In reality, people are neither wholly irrational nor wholly rational. Neither the state of nature nor the perfect rational community are real possibilities. In the real world, people are rational to some extent, but are affected by their passions to a large extent too. While they see that it is to their advantage to live together and help one another, their affects cause them to come into conflict: a civil state and the rule of law are needed to prevent people from harming one another and to promote social harmony. For Spinoza, the state exists to manage the behaviour of people who are prone to act on their affects. The only way to restrain affects is by the use of stronger affects (P7), so the state prevents people acting from anger and hatred by making them feel stronger affects of fear. The state creates laws based on its estimation of good and evil, and causes its population to associate disobedience with fear of punishment.

The system of civil laws is based on the association of images with affects. Civil laws are therefore 'imaginary'. They do not necessarily reflect what is truly good and bad for human nature; they are a set of universal laws that represent what the community imagines to be good and bad for it. Civil laws are necessary fictions, for they moderate the affects of irrational people and can promote their virtue. At their best, civil laws coincide with true laws of human nature (as in the law against murder, for instance). At their worst, civil laws are based on religious doctrine, which relies on imaginary associations of human activities with transcendent values of good and evil (the law against homosexuality, still in place in a number of countries, is one example of a bad law on Spinoza's terms). Spinoza is a strong advocate of the absolute separation of civil laws from religion.

The worst civil states are governed with little rational understanding, enforcing obedience through fear and violence. Such states are likely to be authoritarian, repressive and belligerent, and prevent the flourishing and rational understanding of their people. Bad states may be led by tyrants, religious zealots or leaders blinded by ideology, hatred or greed. Ultimately, such states can only spiral downwards as their people are further enslaved to affects and images. Better civil states, by contrast, are guided by rational understanding, with a view to increasing citizens' understanding and virtue. A rational leader keeps people's affects in check through the use of stronger affects, but also promotes liberty, tolerance, peace and the pursuit of knowledge. As its people become more rational, they require less state control. Because we build rational understanding when we work together, the best society is one in which a *group* of rational people combines forces to determine its laws: a democracy.

Since the state's judgement of what is 'good' and 'evil' is largely imaginary, notions of justice and injustice, sin and merit, are imaginary too. People's actions are just or unjust, punishable or praiseworthy, only in relation to the laws of the state. Although Spinoza does not mention it here, it is clear that the state requires another fiction, the notion of *free will*, in order to punish people for their wrongdoing and praise them for their obedience. The legal system works on the principle that only a person who freely intended a wrong act should be punished for it. Free will and intentions are necessary fictions employed to make people responsible and accountable for their actions.

Spinoza's Ethics of Joy

In the next set of propositions (P38–58), Spinoza sets out some ethical principles that follow from his definitions of good and evil (D1, D2), his definition of virtue (D8) and the connection of virtue with power, activity and reason.

Anything that truly contributes to our flourishing and increases our activity is good. So whatever we encounter that enhances our minds' and bodies' capabilities – books, sports, the company of friends – is good, while anything that makes us incapable of greater activity – biting insects, sickness, aggressive neighbours – is evil (P38). Those things that preserve our body's proportion of motion and rest, such as the food and water that keep the body going at the same rate, are good (P39). Things that change the body's proportion of motion and rest are evil, because such changes, in transforming the body, weaken or destroy it. A person who knocks you out, a drug that causes your heart rate to speed up to a dangerous level, a venomous snake bite, a disease that impedes your movement: all are evil, because they cause the body's parts to have a different proportion of motion and rest to one another, threatening to break up the constitutive relation that is the essence of your body. If all the body's parts acquire a different proportion of motion and rest, the individual is entirely transformed, which is how Spinoza defines death. Death does not require the body to be 'changed into a corpse' (P39S). Death is always the transformation, never the absolute cessation, of being. (We shall return to this point in Part V.)

Things that preserve our being and enhance our living are *ethically* good, they make us feel *joy*. 'Joy is an affect by which the body's power of acting is increased or aided' and is good in itself (P41). Sadness, by contrast, is an affect by which the body's power of acting is diminished and is directly evil (P41). Everything that brings us joy is good. But the affects of joy can be excessive. Bodily pleasure can preoccupy us with one part of the body to the detriment of our whole being (P43). Love and desire, too, can make us focus obsessively on the joy we get from one person or thing and neglect other things that are good for us (P44). We should strive for that joy that reflects the well-being of all the parts of the body together, which Spinoza calls cheerfulness (P42).

Hatred of people, in all its variants, is necessarily evil (P45). For hatred makes us strive to destroy another person, which is contrary to virtue (according to P37). Affects related to hatred – envy, mockery, disdain, anger and vengeance – are similarly evil (P45C1). Can anger not be a positive feeling, spurring us on to challenge injustice and improve our lives and communities? It can, but on Spinoza's account, your positive action does not arise from anger as such. Rather, you have rationally understood your anger and its causes, thereby transforming it from a passion that acts on you to an action that you control. (This process will be explained in 'Part V: Freedom and Eternity'.)

Spinoza makes a point of noting that laugher, joking and pleasure are ethically good. To forbid yourself pleasure is to be under a 'savage and sad superstition' (P45S). Spinoza's target here is the religious morality (of Calvinism in particular) that proclaims the moral depravity of joy and pleasure and the moral goodness of meekness and despondency. Why, Spinoza asks, is it deemed acceptable to relieve our hunger and thirst with food and drink, but not to relieve our melancholy with joy? Joy is the affirmation of our flourishing and our virtue. Any religion that claims that joy and pleasure are evil, and that God is pleased by despondency, misunderstands God, does violence to human beings and diminishes their virtue (see also IV App. XXXI). God does not take pleasure in our misfortune. Rather, as we feel more joy, we participate more in the divine nature, because we increase our being and perfection (P45S). The wise man takes pleasure in things in moderation to meet all of the needs of his body and mind:

It is the part of a wise man, I say, to refresh and restore himself in moderation with pleasant food and drink, with scents, with the beauty of green plants, with decoration, music, sports, the theatre, and other things of this kind, which anyone can use without injury to another. For the human body is composed of a great many parts of different natures, which constantly require new and varied nourishment, so that the whole body may be equally capable of all the things which can follow from its nature, and hence, so that the mind also may be equally capable of understanding many things at once. (P45S)

Spinoza's ethics is an ethics of joy. What increases our cheerfulness of body and mind is ethically good. What brings us sadness, impedes our joy and makes us weak of body and melancholy of mind is ethically evil.

An ethics of joy cannot accommodate the sad passions. So hope, fear, pity, humility and repentance cannot be ethically good (P47, P50, P53, P54). Christian morality is based on sad passions: fear of God, the guilt of sin, the requirement to act out of pity, repentance for one's misdeeds and the hope for salvation. Two hundred years after Spinoza's death, Nietzsche would call it 'slave morality': the morality that valorises weakness, meekness and passivity over power, self-love and activity. Spinoza and Nietzsche both believe that Christian morality has ethics backwards. It falsely associates virtue with affects of humility and repentance, such that people believe it is *good* to lack power. For Spinoza, to believe that guilt, repentance and humility are *good* is to be enslaved to the sad passions. Spinoza and Nietzsche both advocate an ethics of joy, based on the power and activity of the human mind and body.

Spinoza accepts, however, that humility and repentance are useful for social cohesion. It is better that irrational people should be humble and fearful than proud and unafraid (P54S). He suggests that the prophets, including Jesus Christ, were rational leaders who guided people towards virtue through affects of humility and repentance (P54S). At its core, Spinoza sees Christianity as a rational way of organising irrational people. It is a fiction, but like the legal system, it is useful and desirable for promoting good behaviour. But when it proclaims a false morality, diminishing people's virtue, impeding their reason and preventing them from acting according to their own nature, religion becomes a force of enslavement and superstition.

We can see why Spinoza believes fear, humility and repentance are ethically bad. But what about pity? Pity often moves us to do what is ethically good. But Spinoza insists that 'pity, in a man who lives according to the guidance of reason, is evil of itself and useless' (P50). This is because pity is a sadness. If you help someone out of pity, then you are being led by your affects. Your action may have good results and it may make you feel good too, but it is not *virtuous*, because it was not determined by the laws of your own nature. (Kant later makes a very similar point in his *Groundwork for the Metaphysics of Morals*.) The rational person knows with certainty that helping another person is ethically good and helps from the laws of his own nature. He does not feel pity for the other person's suffering, for he knows that it follows from the necessity of the divine nature. Such a person 'finds nothing worthy of hate, mockery, or disdain, nor anyone whom he will pity. Instead, he will strive, as far as human virtue allows, to act well, as they say, and rejoice' (P50S).

Of course, Spinoza is not suggesting that the rational person rejoices at other people's suffering. He is saying that the rational person accepts that the suffering, like all things, is necessary and strives not to let that fact diminish his own being. Instead of feeling pity for the suffering, he feels the joy of his ability to help. Like humility and repentance, pity can be useful in spurring irrational people on to do the right thing. It is, of course, better to help someone from pity than not to help them at all (P50S). But it is best is to help someone from the laws of one's own nature: only then is one's action truly virtuous.

Some affects are compatible with reason, namely, those that make us feel *active joy*: the joy we feel when we are the adequate cause of our actions. Passive joy (from external things) is good and increases our virtue, but only to a certain extent. A person who desires only the passive joys of food and drink, for instance, will flourish when those desires are satisfied, but his flourishing will easily be diminished if those things are absent. Furthermore, his rationality and activity will increase only minimally, because the images and affects of food and drink govern his thinking and his acting.

Active joy, by contrast, does not depend on external things, but arises when we act from our own nature. Active joy takes the form of 'noble' affects that are compatible with reason: love, favour and self-esteem. In this state we strive most strongly not to feel the sad passions of hatred or anger, and since these feelings come about most often from other people's hatred and anger, we strive that they should not be troubled by sad passions either. It is to our own advantage to repay the other's hatred with love (P46), for love can destroy hatred (IIIP43). When we are most rational we favour those who are virtuous (P51) and take joy in our own power of acting (P52). This rational self-esteem should not be confused with pride. Whereas pride arises from one's false *image* of one's own deeds, rational self-esteem comes about with true knowledge of one's virtue (see P57 and P58). The virtuous person is not meek or self-effacing, as Christian morality would have it. He perceives his power clearly and distinctly and takes joy in his virtue.

At the end of 'Part II: Minds, Bodies, Experience and Knowledge' I suggested that the *Ethics* sets us a project of becoming more rational and thereby recovering our true essence. As we gain more adequate ideas, we regain more and more true understanding of our essence, and we *act* from our essence. When we act from our essence, we are virtuous and powerful. We do what is truly good for us and what is truly good for all humanity. So, *to know our own essence* is of primary importance for living an ethical life. This is suggested in P55 and P56, where Spinoza argues that very great pride and very great despondency involve 'very great ignorance of oneself' and 'very great weakness of mind'. In extreme pride and extreme despondency, our minds are overtaken with a false image of ourselves, preventing us from knowing or acting from our essence. A person entirely alienated from his own essence is extremely weak, passive and evil. To regain understanding of our essence is to regain our power: the more we accomplish this, the better and happier we will be.

Good and Evil Actions

Up to now, our understanding of what is ethically good and evil has been based on *things* that are good or bad for us. A couple of problems may have occurred to you. First, if things are good or evil only from the perspective of the individual, how do we solve ethical problems involving different perspectives? Second, shouldn't the terms 'good' and 'evil' be applied to actions, such as generosity and murder, rather than to things, such as food and hurricanes?

To answer the first question, let us return to an earlier example. Displacing a fishing community to build a hotel is evil for the fishermen and good for the developers. Who is right? On the one hand, both parties are, because what is good for the flourishing of one is bad for the flourishing of the other. But on the other hand, if both parties had full rational understanding, they would agree about what in this situation was best for the flourishing of all humanity. So there must be some truth about what is best, which can be discovered through reason. From a Spinozist perspective, all ethical problems have solutions that are immanent within our shared human nature. But because we are not 100% rational, we seldom know the answers with certainty. That is why we continue to have moral disputes. Our best hope for solving moral problems is to continue to work together to build our rational understanding.

The second question is more complex. Spinoza certainly believes that 'good' and 'evil' apply to our actions as much as they do to the things we encounter. But how do we determine the ethical status of an action? As you might expect, a good action is one that is determined by our own nature, through rational understanding. An evil action is one that is determined by our passions, based on external causes. In other words, an action's ethical status does not depend on what kind of action it is. Rather, it depends on *how the action is caused*.

This means that any action can be a good action, so long as we are the adequate cause of it. Anything that we are determined to do by our passions and which is evil can equally be determined by reason and be good. This is what Spinoza is saying in P59: 'to every action to which we are determined from an affect which is a passion, we can be determined by reason, without that affect'. In other words, there are no actions that are *only* determined by our affects, and therefore there are no actions that are purely evil. That is because the affects only diminish our power of acting: they do not give us the power to do things that are not in our nature. Every action that we undertake is part of our nature, but these actions become highly confused and inadequate when they are determined through the passions. Every action that is confused and evil can also be 'unconfused' and good if it is determined by reason. 'No action, considered in itself, is good or evil . . .; instead, one and the same action is now good, now evil. Therefore, to the same action which is now evil . . . we can be led by reason' (P59 Alt. Dem.).

This seems to have some very disturbing consequences. Spinoza appears to be saying that actions such as murder, rape and torture are not evil in themselves, but are evil because they are determined by the passions. Is Spinoza really saying that these actions could equally be determined by reason and be *good*?

We need to consider this carefully. Spinoza is indeed denying that any action is evil in itself. Murder is evil because the person who undertakes it is determined by anger and hatred. If that person were not determined by his passions and determined by reason instead, then his action would have virtue. But if he were truly determined by reason, this person's action *would not be murder*. Consider what 'murder' is, on Spinoza's account. It involves the action of pulling a gun's trigger, combined with a feeling of extreme hatred connected to the image of another person. If the feeling of hatred and the image of the other person are removed, then *only the action* remains. The action of pulling a gun's trigger is not *in itself* evil; considered simply as a movement of the body, it is an action of the body and it is *good*. It only becomes evil and becomes murder when this action is determined by affects and images. So this man could be determined by rational understanding of his own nature to pull the trigger, thus actualising a bodily capability. But reason could *only* determine him to do this in circumstances where nobody would be harmed (such as a shooting range), because destroying another person is contrary to reason.

Read the scholium to P59. Spinoza gives us the example of a man making a punching action with his arm. If the idea of his arm's action is caused by his mind's adequate idea of the structure of his body, this man understands his body rationally and is the *adequate cause* of the punching action. He fully causes the effect, alone, from adequate ideas. This action, considered on its own, is a virtue: it is an increase of the man's capabilities and power. That same action would be an *evil* action if it were inadequately understood and inadequately caused. If the same man is preoccupied by the image of his neighbour and he punches his neighbour from anger, he is the *inadequate cause* of the punching action. His behaviour is determined by his passions, lacks virtue and is evil.

In other words, every evil action is a confusion or perversion of some activity that follows from our nature, just as every false idea is a confusion or perversion of a true idea that is part of our mind. And so every evil action, if the passions are removed and the action is clearly understood in itself, can be good. Spinoza is *not* saying that murder, rape or torture can be good. Rather, he is saying that at their core, these actions involve activities of our bodies that are good (pulling a trigger, sexual activity, sharing knowledge), but become evil when they are determined by anger, hatred and cruelty rather than reason. Reason determines us to exercise these bodily activities *only* in ways that cause no harm to others. A person who harms another is necessarily determined by passions and his action is necessarily evil. (On this, see also VP4S.)

In Spinoza's system there is no 'force for evil' and no one has an 'evil nature'. 'Knowledge of evil is inadequate knowledge' (P64): evil is not part of anyone's essence and it cannot be truly understood. True understanding applies only to being. Evil, like falsity, has no being. It is not a mode of God, but the confusion of God's modes. As the lack of adequacy of thinking and acting, evil is the *privation of good*.

Even with this explanation, you may find Spinoza's point here very difficult to accept. There are some actions which are so evil that it is impossible to see how they can be based on any 'good' activity or how they could be made 'good' if the passions were removed. Spinoza's view that evil is merely the confusion or privation of good is particularly difficult to accept given the extreme evils that humans caused one another in the twentieth century. It is for this reason that some readers find Spinoza too much of a cold rationalist who unrealistically rejects the positive ways that feelings can guide our moral action and judgement.

Free Will and Moral Responsibility

A person is evil because he is the inadequate cause of his actions, making him bad for his own flourishing and the flourishing of others. Evil actions decrease his virtue: in doing something that harms another person, he does something contrary to his own advantage. The person who does evil is at a low point of rationality and activity, lacking understanding of himself and heavily influenced by forces outside him.

The evil person is not *responsible* for his badness; rather, he is *weak* of body and mind. His body is overly affected by external things, and his mind is taken up by inadequate ideas. Lacking understanding of his own nature, he will inevitably have more bad experiences than good ones and will be very easily swayed by sad passions of hatred, resentment, anger and fear. He lives irrationally and weakly, relying on external things for fleeting, passive joys, directed by his affects and never knowing himself adequately.

This raises another troubling point: it appears that the evil person is not responsible for his actions. As we know, Spinoza denies that people have free will. No person is the absolute cause of his actions and so no person is absolutely responsible for what he does. As we have seen, we are *least* responsible for our actions when we are least virtuous. It seems that we can get away with evil acts on the grounds that 'my affects made me do it'. Every person who does something evil, it seems, can appeal to a version of the insanity defence: we are not responsible for our crimes because our minds and bodies are not under our own control.

Furthermore, if there is no free will, it seems that becoming virtuous is simply a matter of fate and chance. The person who has had good encounters in life and who has not suffered much sadness will be troubled by few powerful affects and will more easily achieve reason and virtue. By contrast, a person who has had a difficult time in life, ground down by wars, violence and poverty, will become rational and virtuous only with great difficulty, for he will be strongly affected by his experiences. Is becoming virtuous just a matter of good luck, an accident of birth?

These objections were made to Spinoza by his correspondent E.W. von Tschirnhaus. He felt that if we have no free will, it would be impossible to acquire the habit of virtue and 'all wickedness would be excusable' (Letter 57, CW 907). Spinoza's response is unequivocal:

> I do not know who has told [you] that we cannot be of strong and constant mind from the necessity of fate, but only from free will. As to [your] final remark, that 'on this basis all wickedness would be excusable', what of it? Wicked men are no less to be feared and no less dangerous when they are necessarily wicked. (Letter 58, CW 910)

We do not need the concept of free will to explain a person's virtue or lack of virtue. People are good or evil not by choice or intention, but by necessity. What does it matter, Spinoza says, if the murderer is not *responsible* for his wickedness? Nobody is disputing that this man *caused* another person to die. It is just that he did not cause it *freely* or *intentionally*. He was necessitated to do it by the external causes acting on him, but he is no less dangerous, fearful or bad for that. His lack of moral responsibility does not absolve him from punishment. Indeed, he must be punished so that stronger affects of fear and pain will prevent him murdering again. The legal system makes him accountable for the effects he has caused, but such accountability is ultimately a fiction (albeit a necessary one). The murderer *causes* the victim's death, but he is not *morally responsible* for it – just as a tsunami causes, but is not morally responsible for, destroying a village.

Similarly, a person is not virtuous through free choice. A person who teaches a group of impoverished children to read, for instance, is the *cause* of her own increased virtue and of theirs, but she did not *freely choose* it. Rather, she is necessitated to choose it by her nature alone. She understands her own nature rationally and knows that teaching children is good, both for herself and for humanity, and her nature determines her to do it. Both the good and bad person are necessitated to do what they do. But whereas the bad person is necessitated by the flux of external things, the good person is necessitated by her nature alone.

Given Spinoza's denial of free will, is there any point in trying to be virtuous? Yes there is, because *determinism* – acknowledging that all our actions have causes – does not amount to a *fatalism*, where all our actions are set in advance. We shall explore this distinction in 'Part V: Freedom and Eternity'.

Reason, Virtue and Freedom

Spinoza closes Part IV with some propositions on 'the free man'. The free person is one who is not enslaved to affects, and is rational and active. He 'complies with no one's wishes but his own, and does only those things he knows to be the most important in life, and therefore desires very greatly' (P66S).

Why does Spinoza say that this person is *free*? Not because he has free will, to be sure, but rather because this person is determined to act by his nature alone. Look back at Spinoza's definition of freedom at ID7: 'that thing is called free which exists from the necessity of its nature alone, and is determined to act by itself alone.' In Part I, we saw that only God is free in an absolute sense, because only God is the cause of its own existence. But finite modes can be free too, in a relative sense. They do not cause their own existence, but they can become the adequate cause of the effects that follow necessarily from their nature. In causing their own effects, they are determined to act by themselves alone, free of external influence. To use a different philosophical idiom, the free person is *autonomous*. Self-determination does not mean acting from free will; it means being determined by our true 'self', our essence.

The free person understands rationally and acts virtuously. She is not led to act by the pleasures of the moment (P62) or by fear (P63). When faced with ethical problems, she weighs up goods and evils to determine which is best: she follows the greater of two goods or the lesser of two evils (P65). She sacrifices a lesser present good for a greater future good and prefers a lesser present evil to a greater future evil (P66). She avoids danger and the favours of the irrational (P69, P70) and acts with honesty and honour (P71, P72). The rational person understands that it is better for her to live in a state and abide by its laws than to live in solitude (P73). She strives to increase the rationality of others, so they live according to the command of their own reason, and not according to the forces of superstition (IV App. IX).

The rational, virtuous person does not imagine that he or anyone does anything out of free choice; he therefore feels no guilt, blame or pride. He does not resent things that turn out badly for him or hate people who do him harm. Most importantly, he has true understanding of his own nature and of his place in the universe. He understands that he is a finite mode of infinite God, that all things follow from the necessity of the divine nature,

and hence, that whatever he thinks is troublesome and evil, and moreover, whatever seems immoral, dreadful, unjust, and dishonourable, arises from the fact that he conceives the things themselves in a way which is disordered, mutilated, and confused. (P73S)

The free person understands that village-destroying tsunamis, mass murderers, malaria-spreading mosquitoes and deformity-causing chemicals follow from the necessity of the divine nature and that, from God's perspective, these things are neither evil nor good. He knows that they are evil only from his own finite, inadequate perspective, and that if he could see the world from God's perspective, he would not be troubled by them. He strives, therefore, to understand things as best he can, to avoid being affected by evil things, 'to act well, and rejoice' (P73S).

The free person is determined by his nature to preserve his life and to enhance his living. He understands his own power, strives to actualise it and rejoices in it. His 'wisdom', then, is an understanding of his life and power, and he does not preoccupy himself with death. 'A free man thinks of nothing less than of death, and his wisdom is a meditation on life, not on death' (P67).

If people are like waves on the sea, tossed about by contrary winds, then the free person is one who strives not to be affected by being tossed about, who strives to understand his position as a wave on the sea. It is clear that no human being can be *entirely* free, because we are necessarily determined by other things to some extent. Nor is anybody born free (P68). We cannot be entirely unaffected by the evils that befall us, but understanding our own power will enable us to bear those evils calmly. The extent to which this is possible is explored in Part V.

Human power is very limited and infinitely surpassed by the power of external causes. . . . Nevertheless we shall bear calmly those things which happen to us contrary to what the principle of our advantage demands, if we are conscious that we have done our duty, that the power we have could not have extended itself to the point where we could have avoided those things, and that we are a part of the whole of nature, whose order we follow. (IV App. XXXII)

How, then, does Spinoza's ethics relate to Spinoza's *Ethics*? Ethics, for Spinoza, is not based on transcendent values or moral laws; it is immanent to the nature of individuals. The right way to live is based on understanding what we are, on understanding and doing what is good for our being. Because ethics is grounded in the nature of being, and because acting well is grounded in true understanding, it was necessary to understand what being is (Part I); and how we can know it (Part II), before we could understand how we should live (Part IV). Part IV closes with an Appendix which summarises Spinoza's ethical ideas.

Part V: Freedom and Eternity

Part V is the final part of the *Ethics* and is also its most contested. It is split roughly in two. The first half (P1–20), in which Spinoza completes his discussion of ethics and freedom, is continuous with Parts III and IV and is unproblematic, though it poses some difficult ideas. But the second half (P21–42) is truly puzzling. On the one hand, it completes the *Ethics* by bringing us full circle, back to the ontology of Part I. But in doing so, it seems to call into question many of the naturalistic ideas that Spinoza argues for in other parts of the book. In Part V, Spinoza appears to argue for the immortality of the mind after death, God's infinite love for us and our potential for intuition, the mysterious 'third kind' of knowledge.

Critics have been sharply divided about how to interpret Part V and have even questioned whether we should take it seriously. Bennett, for instance, calls it 'an unmitigated and seemingly unmotivated disaster' (1984: 357). I do not share this view. To be sure, Part V contains obscurities, problems and apparent contradictions, leaving the interpreter without a clear route through. But in reading it, one gets a sense of how Spinoza meant its propositions to follow from ideas advanced in the other parts of the *Ethics* (even if they fail to do so when subjected to critical scrutiny). I see no great mystery about Spinoza's motivation for discussing the eternal existence of the mind and the third kind of knowledge. Spinoza needs to say something about our eternal being in order to complete the metaphysical system of the *Ethics*. The impossibility of giving a coherent account of eternity – as evinced by the incoherence of VP21–42 – is productive in that it reveals something interesting about what a finite mode can and cannot do. Perhaps the second half of Part V should be seen as an experiment in which Spinoza tests the capabilities of his own thinking.

I will not spend any time discussing the issues of interpreting VP21–42. Instead, I will suggest a way of reading that section and briefly indicate some of the problems that arise from it. This is an opportunity for you to critically assess my interpretation against your own or against those of other commentators.

Our Power over the Affects

The title of Part V is 'Of the Power of the Intellect, or On Human Freedom'. Whereas Part IV is about the power of the affects over us, Part V is about the power of the mind, when it understands rationally, over the affects. This power to restrain our affects and to determine ourselves to act is our freedom. In the Preface to Part V, Spinoza reminds us that restraining the affects is not a matter of will (as Descartes supposes). The mind's power does not consist in *willing* the body to do this or that, but rather in *understanding* the body. Freedom from the affects, then, is not a matter of will, but of rational understanding.

How does rational understanding enable us to restrain and moderate the affects? Spinoza explains this process in P1–10. Essentially, he argues, we overcome our passivity to the affects by transforming that passivity into activity. And we gain the power to control our affects by forming adequate ideas of them. We shall go through this argument in detail.

First, we need to remind ourselves of the principle of parallelism (IIP7). For every idea that the mind thinks, there is a parallel event of the body (i.e. it physically acts, or is acted on). And since every idea causes other ideas, every bodily event causes other bodily events, in parallel. This parallelism between ideas of the mind and events of the body occurs whether the ideas are adequate (in which case the body acts) or inadequate (in which case the body is acted on). For this reason, the order and connection of ideas in the mind is parallel to the order and connection of the body's affections (P1).

The great limitation of being a finite mode, as Spinoza has stressed throughout the *Ethics*, is that the order and connection of our ideas and affections is not determined exclusively by ourselves. To a very great extent, that order and connection are determined by the things we interact with. Being 'part of nature' means we are affected, both mentally and physically, by the things we encounter. Our goal is to become more self-determining, so that the order and connection of our ideas and affections are less determined by those external things. If we achieve this, we become free, in the sense that we act from the necessity of our nature alone, no longer determined by our affects (ID7).

So, how do we free ourselves from the affects? Through a method of subtraction and transformation. The key is to separate the affects from the inadequate ideas we have of external causes (P2), and to gain adequate ideas of the affects that remain (P3).[4] For example, hatred is sadness accompanied by the image of an external cause (IIIP13S). If you separate the feeling of sadness from the image of the person you hate, then you will no longer feel hatred, you will just feel sadness. The affect is then solely related to *your body*, which you *can* understand adequately (because you have the potential to understand everything in your body adequately, IIP12). Sadness is a confused idea, for passions are always inadequate ideas (III Gen. Def.). But if you form an adequate idea of the sadness, you understand it truly: it ceases to be a confused idea. It then ceases to be a passion and ceases to be sadness – when it is truly understood, it becomes an action, which is always joyful.

This means that while we cannot prevent external things from affecting us, we can have some control over the bodily changes that result. We have more control over our bodily changes as we gain more adequate knowledge of the body's parts and processes.

---

[4]   Note that Spinoza uses the term 'clear and distinct idea' in P3 and 'clear and distinct concept' in P4. These terms mean the same thing as 'adequate idea'. Every adequate idea is understood *clearly* and *distinctly*, unobscured by, and unconfused with, other ideas.

For as we gain adequate knowledge of those parts and processes, we become the adequate cause of their activity: bodily changes are caused by our body alone, according to the laws of its nature. As we have more adequate knowledge of the affects – which *are* bodily changes – we determine them ourselves, and they become *actions*. To the extent to which we adequately understand the affects and become their adequate cause, they are necessarily joyful and good. In gaining adequate knowledge, we have 'unconfused' our idea of how our body is affected. This process of clarifying an inadequate idea into an adequate one is the clarification of passivity into activity, sadness into joy, evil into virtue, enslavement into freedom.

Our goal, then, is to gain adequate understanding of our bodies and their affects. There is no bodily change of which we cannot form an adequate idea (P4), and therefore there is no affect that we cannot truly understand (P4C). 'Each of us has – in part, at least, if not absolutely – the power to understand himself and his affects, and consequently, the power to bring it about that he is less acted on by them' (P4S). It is therefore crucial that we understand each affect clearly and distinctly. This is the justification for Part III of the *Ethics*: in order to restrain the specific affects of ambition, jealousy, ethnic hatred, and so on, we must understand each one *in its specificity*, clearly and distinctly from the others. The person who has truly understood Part III has gained the adequate knowledge needed to moderate the affects defined there.

Spinoza's programme for restraining our feelings may strike you as unrealistic. It is hard to see how you can overcome your grief at a loved one's death, or your fear of a man pointing a gun at you, simply by *understanding* those feelings. Spinoza accepts that very powerful feelings may be impossible to restrain. But even where true understanding cannot overcome the affects entirely, it helps us to manage them. In extreme fear, you act more rationally if you are able to separate your feelings from the situation and keep them under control. Furthermore, better understanding of ourselves helps us to cope better with emotional problems, as common-sense emotional advice tells us. When a friend suffers a painful break-up, we advise them to 'work through' their feelings: healing comes from clarifying one's emotional state and regaining control over one's feelings and actions. Numerous forms of therapy advise that happiness is best achieved by understanding the causes of unhappiness and gaining control over how they affect us.

Gaining true understanding of our affects not only diminishes their power over us; it makes us act more virtuously too. Feelings and desires determine us to act badly only insofar as they arise from inadequate ideas. But when our desires are truly understood, they are adequate ideas of what our nature truly desires, which determine us to act well. A desire for money may cause a person to act dishonestly, for instance, but when the desire is 'unconfused' from its external cause, it is truly understood to be a rational desire for well–being, determining the person to seek only enough money to ensure cheerfulness, without disadvantage to others. His inadequately understood desire is clarified as the virtuous desire that it fundamentally is (see IVP59), and his evil actions are clarified into good ones.

The mind has its greatest power over the affects when it understands that all things are necessary (P6), for we understand the causes by which things are determined to act. We no longer imagine that anyone acts from free choice, significantly reducing the emotional impact of their actions. When we understand that all things are necessary, we feel neither overestimation nor resentment, neither pride nor blame. We neither envy those with power nor pity those who are powerless. When we understand that bad events could not have been otherwise, we are less powerfully saddened by them. This is where the therapeutic power of reading the *Ethics* reveals itself: the person who has truly understood Spinoza's argument for determinism in Part I is far more capable of moderating her feelings, is more powerful and more free.

Freedom within Determinism
Our mind's essence is a certain sequence of ideas in the infinite intellect: ideas of the same sequence of actions in motion and rest. When we regain some of those ideas and cause the corresponding actions, we get back on track with our essence. Instead of acting according to what affects us (which Spinoza sometimes calls 'the common order of nature'), we act according to the order of the infinite intellect. This is what Spinoza means by 'following the laws of your own nature', and this, for him, is freedom.

Spinoza expresses this in the following way in P10: 'So long as we are not torn by affects contrary to our nature, we have the power of ordering and connecting the affections of the body according to the order of the intellect.' Provided that we are not completely overpowered by sad passions (in which case we lack the power to determine ourselves), we are capable of determining the order and connection of our own bodily changes, according to the order of adequate ideas.

But this proposition seems to lead to a problem. Spinoza has just reminded us that all things in nature happen necessarily (P6). Surely it cannot be that we freely *choose* how to order and connect our bodily affections, or that we are *responsible* for aligning our bodily affections with the order of adequate ideas. If our actions are necessarily determined, how is it that we also have the potential to 'order and connect' our activities? How do we reconcile Spinoza's determinism with his claim for self-determination and his denial of free will with his affirmation of freedom?

In P10, Spinoza is not saying that we freely choose how to order and connect the affections of the body. Our freedom does not consist in the ability to make free choices. But it is important to see that Spinoza's denial of free will is not a denial that we make choices or cause events. You chose to read this book and you caused the book to be picked up and opened. Spinoza does not deny any of this, but he does deny that your choices and acts originate in your will, uncaused by anything else. There can be no acts that *originate absolutely* in the human will: rather, every act, every choice, is necessarily determined by an infinite chain of causes (IP28, IIP48). Since 'the will and the intellect are one and the same' (IIP49C), our choices are not different from the other ideas we think. Choices are ideas determined by other ideas in the mind, with parallel actions determined by physical events in the body.

For this reason, our choices are caused in just the same way as other ideas are caused: in the mind, they follow from a sequence of thinking, and in the body, from a parallel sequence of acting. Our choices may be determined by external causes or by the laws of our own nature. In both cases your choice has been caused, and that cause has been caused by another cause, and so on to infinity (IP29): every choice is fully determined. But a fully determined choice can also be *free*, if it is determined by the ideas and actions that are part of your own nature.

To choose freely, for Spinoza, is to be caused to affirm an idea by those ideas that are immanent to your own nature: the adequate ideas that make up the essence of your mind. When you choose freely, you are unfolding and affirming an adequate idea that was already part of your mind's essence. And, in parallel, you are unfolding and affirming an activity that was already part of your body's constitutive relation. When you chose to pick up this book – assuming you did so freely, unaffected by passions – you affirmed an adequate idea of your body's capability to pick up an object. That adequate idea followed from other adequate ideas in your mind: the adequate idea of your body's extension, the adequate idea of your body's degree of motion, the adequate idea of your arm's ability to move itself, and so on.

'Ordering and connecting the affections of the body according to the order of the intellect' (P10) means that your body acts and changes according to this order of adequate ideas immanent to your essence. To the extent that you do order and connect your affections in this way, your body is less affected and less caused to act by external things. Your 'power' to order and connect your bodily affections is not the power of freely willing your body to do things; it is the power of being the adequate cause of those things that your essence determines you to do. Freedom is the affirmation of your own determination through the necessity of the divine nature.

When they reach this stage of the *Ethics*, many students respond with the question: *what's the point of making choices?* If freedom is nothing but affirming what we are determined to be, our lives seem to be nothing more than the playing-out of a story that has already been written. Does Spinozism necessarily entail fatalism? We shall return to this question at the end of this section.

Freedom, Morality and Love of God

P10 tells us that we can get 'back on track' with our essence, living our lives according to our own nature, rather than the flux of encounters and experiences. But we are capable of attaining only a degree of freedom. Perhaps this is more accurately described as our attaining moments of freedom: we act freely on those occasions when we manage to restrain our affects. We cannot be entirely free, just as we cannot be entirely rational or entirely virtuous. If you could be fully free, you would be wholly self-determining: nothing could affect or destroy you, and you would live and flourish forever. No finite mode can ever achieve this, since finite modes necessarily interact with other finite modes, and are necessarily determined by them to some extent. But we must seek as much freedom and self-knowledge as we can, so we may better resist evil affects and acquire the *habit* of virtue (P10S). Given that we cannot avoid evil affects altogether, Spinoza advocates the practical exercise of building patterns of living.

This means, first, ordering and connecting our affections according to the order of our essence to the extent to which we are able, and second, using imagination to construct ethical maxims, to commit them to memory and to repeat them until they become habitual (P10S). This shows the importance of imagination for living ethically. While Spinoza abjures the imaginary moral laws that are imposed from external sources, he stresses the value of imagining moral precepts based on the true understanding of our nature. If we conceive these rules well and practise them, we will act well from habit even in those cases where the power of the affects renders us incapable of rational action. Furthermore, our incomplete knowledge of what is good for us should not prevent us from living well. If we focus on *imagining* what is virtuous – considering ethical questions, constructing moral rules and practising good behaviour – we will have more positive experiences that build our joy and activity, such that we *truly* become more virtuous, rational and free.

So we must shake off the bad habits of fearing death, dwelling on vices, criticising others and forever focusing on what is bad in the world. By focusing our minds with gladness on what is good, we rejoice in human virtue and come to understand how every evil action and sad passion can be clarified into the good at its core. Just as experiential imaginings are a ladder towards true knowledge, experiential habits are a ladder towards true virtue. We can make ourselves better people by thinking positively, acting well and seeking joy.

P11–20 set out how the free person relates to God. This is best expressed in P15: 'he who understands himself and his affects clearly and distinctly loves God, and does so the more, the more he understands himself and his affects.' No idea, when it is truly under-stood, can be conceived without God (IP15), so every adequate idea that we have is accompanied by the idea of God. Those adequate ideas are also accompanied by active joy, which means that the free person understands God to be the cause of his joy. The more ade-quate ideas we have, the stronger is the idea of God and the stronger is our love for God.

Our love for God grows with our true understanding. No one can hate God (P18), because our idea of God is necessarily adequate and cannot be accompanied by any kind of sadness. A person who believes he hates God is invariably thinking of an image of God (probably from religion) and does not understand God truly. Even when we understand that God is the cause of our sadness, we feel joy and love. For insofar as we understand God to be the cause of the sadness, we truly understand the sadness and it becomes joy (P18S).

Our love for God is not met by God's love for us, for God experi-ences no affects (P17). God therefore is not jealous, envious or angry; he does not love or hate anyone. Our love of God is the most con-stant of the affects, for it is equivalent to true understanding itself and cannot be destroyed (P20S). Furthermore, the mind's greatest good is knowledge of God (IVP28), for true understanding is what is best for the mind. And so, because we desire others to gain true under-standing, we desire that other people know and love God too (P20). Remembering that God is being, this 'love of God' is a love of being. To love all being, and rejoice in it, is our greatest virtue.

This point is difficult to accept. Bubonic plague, atomic bombs and firing squads are caused through the necessity of the divine nature (P6, P18S); are we really expected to love these things and rejoice at truly understanding that they are caused by God? It is hard to see how anyone could ever rejoice at the knowledge that God caused thousands to die in a war or natural disaster. Perhaps Spinoza would respond that this limitation on our joy is part of our finitude. Our inability to rejoice in every aspect of being reflects our inability fully to understand it. If we find we cannot rejoice in something, we have not truly understood that it was caused through the necessity of the divine nature.

How to Live
So, how should we live our lives? Spinoza has built up the answer through the *Ethics*. We must regain the adequate ideas that are immanent to our essence and live our lives as the unfolding and affirming of those adequate ideas. We regain adequate ideas by building common notions. We build common notions through encounters with compositionally similar things, meaning that we must particularly seek out encounters with rational human beings. But the world includes many non-human things with which we share compositional similarities too, and to maximise our potential for building common notions, we must seek encounters with as many of those things as we can. Spinoza advocates our having a great variety of experiences and experimental encounters with things, provided they are not detrimental to our nature. It is crucial to make our bodies more capable, so our minds may be more capable too.

We must especially seek out things that are good for us: things that contribute to the preservation of our being and bring us overall cheerfulness. Primarily, we must seek the cooperation of other people, which is best achieved in the civil state. We must avoid things that are bad for us: things that are contrary to our nature, that affect us with sad passions and that can harm or destroy us, and excessive joys that detract from our overall well-being. When we are affected negatively by external things, we must endeavour to regain power over our affects by 'unconfusing' them from their external causes and understanding the affects clearly and distinctly, so that the passions constitute 'the smallest part of the mind' (P20S). We must understand that we lack power over some external causes and affects, and try to understand their causes as best we can. We must particularly strive to understand that all things are caused through the necessity of the divine nature: through this understanding we love and rejoice in all being.

As finite modes, our project is to get 'back on track' with our essence: to regain true understanding of ourselves and to act freely from our own nature. If we align our finite existence as far as we can with the true order and connection of ideas and activities that is our essence, we will be more rational, more active, and more free. We will be less affected by our passions, will maximise our physical and thinking capacities and act with greater virtue, and our love for all being and knowledge will increase. Our lives are best directed at 'unconfusing' our minds and bodies from the mess of passions and external things, so that we clearly, distinctly, truly, adequately actualise our essence. As Nietzsche was to say two hundred years later: 'Become what you are' (Nietzsche 2001: 152).

Duration and Eternity

Spinoza concludes his discussion of freedom in P20S by summarising in five points the mind's power over the affects. There is a sense in which the *Ethics* ends here, for we have understood what our virtue and freedom are and how we can attain them. But while the ethical system of the *Ethics* may be finished, the metaphysical system is not yet complete. This is indicated in Spinoza's remark in the final paragraph of P20S: 'With this I have completed everything which concerns this present life. . . . So it is now time to pass to those things which pertain to the mind's duration without relation to the body.'

We cannot help being taken aback by this. After so long persuading us that the mind and the body exist in parallel, is Spinoza suddenly saying that the mind can exist *without relation to the body*? To make matters worse, Spinoza states in P23 that 'the human mind cannot be absolutely destroyed with the body, but something of it remains which is eternal'. Is Spinoza arguing that we have an immortal soul, thereby overturning both his parallelism and his naturalism?

Understanding this difficult material requires us first to understand Spinoza's theory of time. Spinoza has, in fact, left clues to this throughout the *Ethics*, but we have not stopped to pick them up, partly because we did not need to until now, but also because of the sheer difficulty of thinking about time. Nevertheless, Spinoza's basic idea is not hard to grasp. Finite modes exist *durationally*, whereas substance, attributes and immediate infinite modes are *eternal*. That is, the existence of finite modes begins, endures and ends. Substance, its attributes of thinking and extension, and its immediate modes of infinite intellect and infinite motion and rest, are eternal.

But what are eternity and duration? Let's look at their definitions. Eternity is 'existence itself, insofar as it is conceived to follow necessarily from the definition alone of the eternal thing'; it 'cannot be explained by duration or time, even if the duration is conceived to be without beginning or end' (ID8). Eternity, therefore, does not refer to an infinite amount of time, but rather to something outside time.

God is an eternal thing because its existence follows necessarily from its definition (IP19), so the existence of God is outside of time and unconstrained by it.

Finite modes, by contrast, are within time and very much constrained by it. Duration is 'an indefinite continuation of existing' (IID5). It is the endurance of a thing for an amount of time that is not determined by that thing's essence. Finite modes endure without knowledge of the extent of their duration, until some other finite mode puts an end to it (IIP30, IIIP8, IVP3). Given this fundamental difference between eternal and durational existence, how is it that durational, finite modes also exist eternally, as Spinoza states at VP23?

You may find it helpful here to re-read the section on 'Spinoza's universe' in 'Part I: Being, Substance, God, Nature' and to consult Figure 1.5. God exists eternally, as do infinite intellect and infinite motion and rest (the immediate infinite modes) (IP21). Spinoza does not make clear whether the infinite continua of thinking and physicality (the mediate infinite modes) are eternal or durational. This obscurity is unfortunate, for it is a matter of some importance. On the one hand, the mediate infinite modes should be eternal, because they follow from other eternal modes (P22, P23). But, on the other hand, they are the 'faces' in which finite modes play out their duration. Duration must somehow be 'in' the mediate infinite modes. Perhaps Spinoza believes that the mediate infinite modes are eternal modes that *cause* duration, but if so, it is not clear how.

Let's put this difficult problem to one side. However eternal being is supposed to produce duration, the actualisation of substance involves the expression of finite modes in durational existence (IP24). So, what is the status of finite modes that no longer, or do not yet, durationally exist? Here, you may wish to re-read the section on 'Essence and existence' in 'Part II: Minds, Bodies, Experience and Knowledge'. Every finite mode has an essence comprising an idea, in the infinite intellect, of its bodily constitution. Because it is part of the infinite intellect, the essence of every finite mode is eternal. Your essence is part of the eternal being of God and is eternally understood by God. But your essence 'involves neither existence nor duration' (IP24C), so the eternal being of your essence does not imply your actual existence at any given time and does not prescribe the duration of your existence. God eternally comprehends the eternal essences of things, regardless of whether those things exist durationally at any given time (IIP8). So, your essence existed in the infinite intellect for eternity before your birth and will exist in the infinite intellect for eternity after your death. The essences of ancient Egyptian farmers, of children not yet born and of creatures who will have evolved in three million years' time exist in the infinite intellect right now and eternally. All these beings exist *really* but *not actually*: they exist 'virtually', in God's idea, before, after and during the time that they are actualised as finite modes (IIP8C).

It should now be clear what Spinoza means in P22 when he says 'in God there is necessarily an idea that expresses the essence of this or that human body, under a species of eternity'. The meaning of P23 should now be becoming clearer too. For the essence of the human mind *is* eternal: it is an idea of the human body, eternally compre-hended by God in the infinite intellect. That idea does not include the actual existence of the body or anything relating to its duration; it therefore does not include the imaginings, affects, experiences or memories that attach to the individual's durational existence (P21). Instead, the essence of the human mind is the idea of the body's *essen-tial constitutive relation*: the relations of motion and rest that define what the body is and is capable of. It is the idea of that essential relation that is eternal, not the durational body with all its traces of experience.

We still do not fully understand Spinoza's meaning in P23, however. Given parallelism, how is it that the body can be destroyed while the mind remains intact? Look at Figure 5.1, which shows what happens to the individual after death (Figure 5.1 is a variant of Figure 2.2, which you should refer to).

When a human being dies, the body (point D) decomposes, and its constitutive proteins and molecules are merged back into the earth to form new individuals. In metaphysical terms, the body is reintegrated, and its parts redistributed, in the infinite continuum of physicality. The elements of the body do not cease to exist altogether: they simply cease to exist *as that human individual*. That particular finite mode has ceased to endure, because the constitutive relation of its durational body has been destroyed. Death is the decomposi-tion of an individual and the recomposition of its elements into other individuals. Death is therefore the transformation of being, not its absolute cessation (see IVP39S).

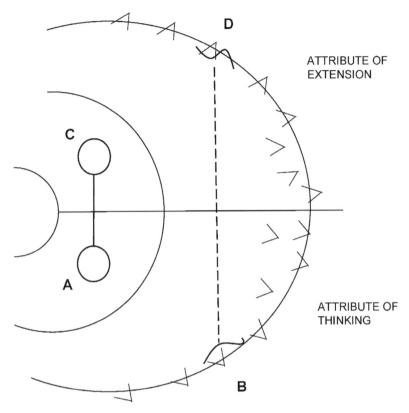

ATTRIBUTE OF
EXTENSION

ATTRIBUTE OF
THINKING

Figure 5.1 The finite individual after death

The durational mind that was the idea of that body (point B) is similarly destroyed and reintegrated into the infinite continuum of thinking. 'An actual mind is nothing but the idea of a singular thing which
actually exists' (IIP11); so when the finite body is destroyed, the finite
mind is destroyed too. Also destroyed is the drive of the individual to
exist as that individual – its conatus. But despite Spinoza's identification of conatus with our essence in Part III, when conatus is destroyed,
something of our essence remains. Points B and D have broken down,
and so relation BD has broken down as well. What remains eternally
here is the idea of the body's essential constitutive relation, AC. The
idea of *what the body essentially is*, is an idea that is eternally true and
cannot be destroyed. *That your body is extended* is conceived through

God's eternal essence (the eternal attribute of extension): it is an eternal truth about your essential nature. There is an order of eternal truths about your essential nature that follow from this one. After your death, your essential nature ceases to be durationally actualised, and therefore these truths cease to be expressed through the individual that you are; but they continue to be true eternally in the infinite intellect.

Parallelism is not threatened by P23, because the parallel between thinking and extension has not been broken. What has been severed is the expressive relation between our essence and our finite existence. Comparing Figures 2.2 and 5.1, what has changed is that AC is no longer *durationally expressed* as BD. But A continues to be parallel to C, and AC continues to exist eternally. *That* is what remains of us before birth and after death.

We cannot remember our eternal being prior to our birth, because experience, memory and duration do not pertain to our eternal being (P23S). But we know rationally that we are eternal and that knowledge affects us with a 'feeling' of our eternity (P23S). We feel that some aspect of ourselves cannot be defined by time, but the confusion of durational existence means that we imagine our eternity as the endurance of our personality after death (P34S). Spinoza's eternity is not a heaven, but the necessary, eternal existence of all things in God.

The Third Kind of Knowledge

All our experience is within durational existence. So when we know through imagination (the first kind of knowledge), we are concerned with the durational aspects of ourselves and other things. We imagine things in relation to certain times and places; we reflect upon our experiences and feel their impact vary according to past, present and future (IIP44S, IVP62S). The separation of time into units – the minutes of the clock and the days of the calendar – is a product of imagination, for it is an abstraction of the duration we experience (IIP44S). But as we gain rational knowledge, we understand more and more that what is true is true eternally, and so we understand reality increasingly 'under a species of eternity' (IIP44C2).

When we know through reason (the second kind of knowledge), we understand that things follow from the necessity of the divine nature, as expressions of God's eternal attributes. We understand things not in terms of how they happen to appear to our senses, but in terms of the essential properties that they share with us: the common notions. Common notions exist in the infinite intellect and are eternally true. For instance, that all physical bodies either move or are at rest (IIA1′) is a common notion. It is true, not at any one particular time, but *eternally*, and that eternal truth is involved in the essence of every physical body. Common notions 'must be conceived without any relation to time, but under a certain species of eternity' (IIP44C2Dem.; see also VP29S).

It is now time for us to consider the mysterious 'third type of knowledge' that Spinoza introduced in Part II: knowledge through intuition. This third type of knowledge was said to 'proceed from an adequate idea of the formal essence of certain attributes of God to the adequate knowledge of the formal essence of things' (IIP40S2). Now, in Part V, Spinoza tells us that this third kind of knowledge is the mind's greatest virtue (P25). What exactly is the third kind of knowledge, and what does Spinoza mean by this?

Spinoza defines intuitive knowledge in terms of a certain direction of thinking: it proceeds *from* an adequate idea of God's attributes *to* adequate knowledge of the essence of things. But rational knowledge (with which we are now familiar) moves in the opposite direction: it proceeds from adequate knowledge of aspects of our own essence to adequate knowledge of God. Intuitive knowledge is therefore something different: it requires a mind that already has an adequate idea of one or more of God's attributes and is capable of deducing the ideas of the essences of things from that adequate idea. For example, such a mind would understand extension fully and truly, and would understand how the essence of a butterfly is fully and truly deduced (or explained) from the nature of extension.

Who could have such a mind? Clearly, God does. God's infinite intellect understands all of reality intuitively: it comprehends *all* of God's attributes and it comprehends perfectly how every essence follows from the nature of those attributes (IIP3). But human beings do not understand reality in this way. Our starting point is the durational world: we gain fragments of knowledge through our experiences, and we gain adequate ideas of some aspects of our own essence through the common notions we are able to build. As we develop our reason, we are increasingly able to acquire and deduce adequate ideas. But the adequate ideas we understand are limited to those that are part of our essence. We truly understand extension, but only insofar as our own essence involves extension. We certainly do not understand extension in a way that would enable us fully to explain the essence of a butterfly.

But Spinoza clearly states that the human mind is capable of intuitive knowledge, and that this is the mind's greatest virtue and joy (P25, P27). Furthermore, he argues that the desire for intuitive knowledge can arise from reason (P28). So how do we move from the second kind of knowledge to the third? This is a matter of considerable debate amongst Spinoza interpreters. I will sketch out here what I think is a plausible reading of P29–31, though I am by no means certain that this is what Spinoza intends.

P29 suggests that there is a fundamental difference between the way we know in our durational existence and the way we know in our eternal existence. While we endure, our knowing necessarily involves duration, for it is constantly conceiving the present existence of the body. No matter how rational we become, and how many adequate ideas we regain, our knowing is structured according to duration. And therefore, while we endure, we can understand rationally that truths are eternal, but we cannot conceive those truths *in an eternal way*. We are capable of understanding that something is eternally true, but we are not capable of conceiving eternally, because as long as we endure, our thinking is necessarily determined in time. Eternity cannot be explained through duration (ID8), and therefore eternity cannot be conceived through durational thinking.

After death, however, the part of us that remains eternally continues to think. Our essential mind conceives the eternal essence of our body. In this respect, our knowing is no longer constrained by time: we conceive eternal truths *in an eternal way*. The essential mind conceives the essential body not insofar as it has present existence, but insofar as it follows from the attribute of extension. In other words, our mind, free of the constraints of duration, no longer needs to use the present body as its starting point for understanding God. The mind moves from understanding *rationally* to understanding *intuitively*. Instead of working from adequate knowledge of our own essence 'upward', as we do when we reason, we proceed from adequate knowledge of God's attributes 'downward'. The mind knows God, and knows itself as it is explained through God's essence (P30).

This seems to me a plausible way of reading P29–31. Spinoza's claim that 'the mind does not have the power of conceiving things under a species of eternity' insofar as it conceives the present existence of its body (P29Dem.) is evidence that the mind cannot understand eternally as long as it endures. P31, which states that the third kind of knowledge depends on the mind 'insofar as the mind itself is eternal', is evidence that the mind is capable of intuitive knowledge only when it is eternal. Finally, there is evidence that an enduring rational being can understand that truths are eternal, but cannot conceive eternally. That evidence comes from Spinoza himself, the enduring rational being who writes P31S. In the final paragraph, Spinoza says that although we are certain that the mind is eternal, in order to understand it, we must 'consider it as if it were now . . . *beginning* to understand things under a species of eternity' (P31S; emphasis added). Clearly, the notion that eternal conceiving *begins* is absurd. But this absurdity is intentional. It is an indication that Spinoza understands *that* the mind is eternal, but cannot conceive things in an eternal way. Neither he nor we can conceive in an eternal way, because we are all durational beings whose thinking is necessarily constrained by time.

For this reason, P32 and P33 are constructed as 'fictions', in which Spinoza *imagines* the mind beginning to think eternally after death (note the words 'feigned' and 'fiction' in P33S). Unlike the first and second kinds of knowledge, Spinoza does not *have* the third kind of knowledge. His writing, in these final ten propositions of the *Ethics*, is therefore strange and incoherent: it reflects the paradox of an enduring rational mind trying to imagine what eternal intuitive knowing must be like.

Blessedness

When a mind knows intuitively and eternally, it takes pleasure in what it understands (P32). But since the mind no longer endures, this pleasure does not involve affects and is not like the pleasures of the finite mind and body. This joy is purely intellectual, encompassing the joy of knowing one's own essence perfectly through that of God. This is what Spinoza calls 'intellectual love of God' (P32C). This is not like love of another person, love of a thing or even the love of God of P15. Intellectual love of God is knowing and loving all being eternally (P33); it is the same love with which God loves itself and all its modes (P35, P36). Since God feels no affects, 'love' is perhaps not the best word; God's love of being is better understood as the affirmation of God's perfection. And it is the affirmation of the perfection of ourselves, in God, that constitutes our blessedness (P36S).

Blessedness consists in the eternal joyful affirmation of intuitively knowing that we are in God and conceived through God. Achieving blessedness means that we truly understand our eternal place in the essence of substance. God, or substance, is pure being, truth, love and affirmative power, and we human beings are a degree of that. Here, Spinoza affirms another key idea of Christian doctrine: the idea that God is love.

P38 and P39 pose serious problems for the interpretation of intuitive knowledge I suggested above. For they suggest that the *extent* of our eternal conceiving varies, depending on the extent to which we have gained rational understanding in duration. The person whose body is more capable, and who knows more rationally, also has a mind 'whose greatest part is eternal' (P39). Given that eternity is not determined by duration, it is difficult to see how the eternity of the mind could grow or shrink in response to our durational developments. Perhaps one way of understanding this is to consider the necessary simultaneity of durational and eternal existence. Because the third kind of knowing is *eternal*, it is necessarily going on even while we endure. So perhaps our eternal conceiving grows *as* we durationally acquire reason. Spinoza suggests, in P38, that the second and third kinds of knowledge grow together, giving this reading some credence. But it remains highly puzzling, since only the second kind of knowledge grows in temporal succession, and it is unclear how the third kind of knowledge grows at all.[5] Nevertheless, Spinoza's meaning seems to be that our eternal knowing increases as we increase our reason and virtue, and therefore that the lives we live do determine the extent of our eternal knowing. It seems, then, that what is 'eternal' can change and be determined by durational existence. The question of how there can be change without time is a perplexing one that cannot be addressed here, except to note Spinoza's

---

[5]   For this reason, some commentators argue that the third kind of knowledge must be possible while we endure, but that reading runs into discrepancies at P29.

likely response: such paradoxes are inevitable when durational minds attempt to imagine eternity.

A life in which we further our capabilities of body and mind, and gain rational knowledge and virtue, is mirrored by our enjoying a greater degree of intuitive understanding and blessedness in eternity. But the rewards of eternity are not what motivate us to live and act well. Even if we were not aware of the mind's eternity, we would know rationally that we must seek our own advantage and act with tenacity and nobility (P41). Freedom and virtue involve a meditation on life, not on death: the motivation for living well is living well itself, not the rewards or punishments we imagine to await us in the afterlife (P41S). Eternity does not come 'after' this life; our eternal blessedness accrues to us as we go. Blessedness, then, is not a reward for living virtuously, but is virtue itself (P42). For the mind's fullest virtue, or power, is attained in eternity, and that power grows as our durational virtue grows.

Here the *Ethics* ends, with Spinoza's famous remarks about the power of the wise person over the ignorant, and about the difficulty of achieving wisdom and power. He assures us that despite its difficulty, each of us is capable of gaining knowledge, virtue, power and freedom. Indeed, by reading and understanding the *Ethics*, we have come a significant way towards our goal.

Is Spinozism Fatalism?

I promised to close the section with a brief discussion of the response that many students have when they finish the *Ethics*: What's the point of making choices, developing adequate ideas, becoming more virtuous, and pursuing freedom, if we are really just playing out whatever God has determined our nature to be? Are all the events of our lives already fated to happen? And if so, how can our freedom make any difference?

Countless commentators have accused Spinoza of being a fatalist – that is, of holding that all our actions are predetermined. And, as we have seen, Spinoza certainly does believe that the essential aspects of our nature are eternally determined in the infinite intellect. But our essence does not involve existence (IP24), so our durational existence and changes are not eternally determined. Because your body's duration is not part of your essence, you cannot gain adequate knowledge of it (IIP30). Not even God has adequate knowledge of your body's duration, insofar as God has the idea of your mind alone. God does have adequate knowledge of your body's duration, but only insofar as God understands the infinite physical continuum as a whole (IIP30Dem.). That is because the precise duration of your body – how long you will live and what will cause you to die – follows from the *entirety* of infinite physical causes. Any actual event of your life can only be *fully explained* by appeal to this infinite network of causes. Only insofar as God comprehends *all* of nature *at once*, does God know how long you will live, what will cause you to die and the other particularities of your actual existence.

Spinoza's God has eternally complete knowledge of everything that happens, has happened and will happen. But from God's perspective, these things do not happen in time, for 'in eternity, there is neither when, nor before, nor after' (IP33S2). God eternally comprehends everything that will happen to you in your future, because from God's perspective, there is no future: all possible events in the universe have already happened (or, rather, they are eternally happening). God cannot decree anything different, for 'God was not before his decrees, and cannot be without them' (IP33S2). There is a sense in which all events in God are eternally fixed and unchanging (as Hegel was later to argue). But, as emphasised above in 'Part I: Being, Substance, God, Nature', God's eternal being is not static. God is self-actualising activity. As God eternally comprehends all events in the universe, God *eternally actualises* them as well. God's eternal being, and eternal activity, is to unfold its own essence eternally.

What this means, for the finite mode, is that there is no question of God 'knowing in advance' what will happen in your life. God has eternal knowledge of every event in the universe. But considered from a durational perspective, God knows the events of your life *as they are actualised* from the divine nature. Those events are fully determined by past events and will go on to determine future events. In this way, your future is indeed determined by the choices you make and the events you cause. You can and do determine the way your life unfolds. You are not a pawn moved around by God or a character in a book God has already written. You are part of God; a mode of God's infinite self-actualisation; a 'surface feature' on the face of substance. The events of your life are not set in advance *for* you, like a road map that you are constrained to follow. They are determined *through* your choices, actions and interactions, every one of which is produced by an infinite nexus of causes.

This should prevent us from taking a fatalistic attitude towards our lives. It is not the case that no matter what you do today you will become a better person because that is your destiny. Nor is it the case that the world will inevitably end up in the same state, regardless of your interventions. You will only become a better person, and the world will only change, if you and others choose to act in ways that will bring those changes about. Determinism does not mean predeterminism, and Spinoza's determinism does not amount to a fatalism. We must act, choose, explore the world, fight injustice, seek joyful encounters and try to become more capable and virtuous beings. Freedom really is worth striving for and really is attainable.

2. Study Aids

Glossary

Spinoza provides definitions of many of his key terms. His definitions, and my explanations of them, can be found through the index to this book. This glossary explains some terms that Spinoza uses, but does not define.

Actualise	To make actual.
Adequate	Complete; containing everything needed to account for that thing. An adequate idea is the complete, true idea of its object and contains all the thinking activity needed to conceive it. An adequate cause is the complete cause of its effect and contains all the physical activity needed to bring it about.
Affections	Changes or properties. In Part I, Spinoza uses 'affections' interchangeably with 'modes', because modes are the changeable properties of substance. In later parts, he speaks of a person's affections, i.e. the changes the body undergoes when it acts or reacts. Be careful to distinguish affections from affects (defined at IIID3 and III Gen.Def.Aff.).
Body	Any physical being. Every body is determined to be what it is by an essential constitutive relation. Every body is known

	by a mind/idea that is strictly parallel to it (IIP7).
'Clear and distinct'	That which is understood completely and on its own. Adequate ideas are understood clearly and distinctly.
Common notion	An idea that is common to the essences of two or more individuals.
Conatus	A being's drive to go on being what it is and to flourish in its being. Sometimes translated as 'striving'. See IIIP6.
Conceive	To understand something truly; to think about something. Conceiving is the activity of the mind (compare with 'perceive').
Concept	In most cases, means the same as 'idea'.
Confused	The state of ideas or bodies when they interact with other ideas or bodies. Also the state of our thinking when it is affected by other ideas.
Contingent	The lack of necessity with which a thing exists. Nothing is truly contingent (IP29), but finite modes call things contingent insofar as their essence neither necessarily posits nor necessarily excludes their existence (IVD3).
Death	The complete breakdown of a body's constitutive relation of motion and rest (and the parallel breakdown of the idea of that body), such that it is transformed into a different body or bodies. See IVP39.
Determinate	(a) The specific way a particular finite mode actualises God's essence (see e.g. IP25C). (b) The specific way a particular finite mode is caused to exist and do things (see IP28). (c) The power of a thing to cause an effect necessarily ('determinate cause': see IA3).
Determine	(a) To specify what a thing is (the essence

of a body is determined through motion and rest, e.g.). (b) To cause a thing to exist, change, act or react (poison determines a body to decrease its activity). All determination is necessary.

Efficient cause

That which produces existence, changes or other effects in something else. God is the immanent efficient cause of all things (IP16C1), whereas finite modes are efficient causes of things and events external to them (IP28).

Essence

What a thing is; what it is to be that thing.

Existence

That a thing is; the actuality of that thing. There is a distinction between eternal existence (of God/substance) and durational existence (of finite modes while they endure).

Expression

The immanent efficient causation of modes by substance.

Extension

Physicality.

Fiction

A coherent set of confused ideas produced in imagination that can delude us (e.g. the Bible), but that can be useful in cases where we lack full rational understanding (e.g. scientific hypotheses and legal systems).

Final cause

That for the sake of which a thing exists or happens. God does not operate according to final causes; all final causes are human fictions (I App.).

Finite mode

A particular thing. A finite mode is a specific, limited expression of one of God's attributes for a certain duration (see IP25C).

Formal being

The actual existence of something (Spinoza uses this term very occasionally, e.g. at IIP5).

Image	The trace left behind on the body and mind resulting from an interaction with another thing; a partial, confused or inadequate idea; the representation of a thing in thinking, language or pictures.
Imagining	The first kind of knowledge: a way of knowing based on the traces of experience. Experiencing, remembering, anticipating, inferring, dreaming and hallucinating are all varieties of imagining. Imagining is the source of empirical knowledge, but also of error and falsity. (NB there is no 'faculty of imagination'.)
Immanent	Internal. 'X is immanent to Y' means that X is within Y, and that Y is ontologically dependent on X. Therefore, X is in Y (where 'in' = within), and Y is in X (where 'in' = dependent on). God is immanent to all things (IP18) means that all things are in God (IP15).
Immediate infinite mode	The infinite expression of God's essence, the existence of which follows immediately and necessarily from the nature of one of God's attributes (IP21).
'In another'	The dependence of something on something else for its being. Modes are 'in' substance, but also, every effect is 'in' its cause.
'In itself'	The dependence of something on itself for its being. Substance alone is 'in' itself.
Inadequate	Incomplete, partial, confused. An inadequate idea is the partially true idea of its object, confused with other inadequate ideas; also refers to confused thinking. An inadequate cause is the partial cause of its effect, confused with other causes. An effect that has been inadequately caused

is not explained fully through that cause and is not fully understood.

Individual

A body comprising a variable number of other bodies that communicate motion to one another at a uniform rate. Individuals are distinguished from one another by different rates of motion, but are only relatively distinct, for the whole of nature is one individual (IIL7S).

Infinite intellect

The immediate infinite expression of the attribute of thinking. Infinite thinking, from which follow all possible ideas and relations of ideas. Infinite intellect contains God's ideas of every one of an infinite number of things in an infinite number of attributes (and the ideas of those ideas, and the ideas of *those* ideas, to infinity).

Infinite motion and rest

The immediate infinite expression of the attribute of extension. Infinite dynamism, from which follow all possible dynamic relations and all possible ways of physical being.

Intuition

The third kind of knowledge, which proceeds from adequate knowledge of God's attributes to adequate knowledge of the essences of things (IIP40S2). Intuiting can be performed only by a non-durational mind (on my interpretation; see 'Part V: Freedom and Eternity').

'Laws of one's own nature'

The order and connection of ideas of the body that constitutes the essence of the mind. When a finite mind regains adequate knowledge of one of these ideas, it is able to deduce a sequence of ideas that follow from it; in parallel, the body acts according to that sequence. This individual acts according to the laws of its nature. It necessarily does what its essence determines to be good for its being.

Mediate infinite mode
The infinite expression of God's essence, the existence of which follows from the nature of an immediate infinite mode (IP22).

Mind
The true idea of a body, comprised of multiple true ideas of the parts and activities of that body. In its essence, those ideas are clear and distinct, and unfold according to a determinate order. In durational existence, those ideas are partial and confused with ideas of other things, and they unfold according to its encounters with those things.

Motion and rest
See infinite motion and rest.

Nature
This term is used in three senses. (a) When capitalised ('God or Nature'), it refers to God or substance, i.e. being as such. (b) As an uncapitalised noun, it refers to the world of finite beings. (c) When it modifies another noun ('the nature of a horse', 'laws of its nature'), it means the essence of a thing, or the essential aspects that a thing shares with others of the same kind ('human nature').

Notion
Usually means the same as concept or idea.

Objective being
The being of something in God's idea, but not in actual existence. This meaning is contrary to our contemporary usage of 'objective', leading to potential confusion; fortunately, Spinoza uses it rarely (e.g. at IIP8C).

'Order and connection'
The order according to which ideas (and, in parallel, actions) follow from one another. In the infinite intellect, and in adequate understanding, ideas are

connected in logical order. In the world of finite things, and in inadequate understanding, ideas (i.e. images) are connected according to the order of experience. Our goal is to isolate our ideas and activities from our experience, and to connect them according to the order of the intellect (see VP10).

Perceive
The thinking activity that the mind is determined to do by something else. Perceiving indicates that something else acts on the mind and body, and that the mind and body are affected by it (sensing is a variant of perceiving).

Perfection
The being, or essence, of a thing, and the completeness with which that thing's being, or essence, is actualised. (a) God is absolutely perfect because its essence is infinite and its essence entails the necessity of its complete actualisation. A finite mode is never absolutely perfect, but can become more perfect as it actualises its essence to a greater extent through increasing its power (see IIIP11S). (b) We judge things more or less perfect in relation to one another insofar as, from our perspective, they have more or less being (IVPref.).

Possibility
There is no possibility in Spinoza's system; all real things are necessary, and all non-real things are impossible. Finite modes use the term 'possibility' in reference to something which is contingent and whose determinate cause is uncertain (IVD4).

Power
The essence of a thing; its ability to actualise itself. Also a finite mode's capacity for mental and bodily activity.

Reality
See Perfection, above ('By reality and

perfection I understand the same thing'; IID6). 'Reality' is not equivalent to 'Actuality'. Anything that has being, or essence, is *real;* some real things are actual (i.e. those that exist durationally), and some real things are not actual (those that no longer, or do not yet, exist durationally). In this book, when I use 'reality' in the conventional sense to mean 'everything that is', I mean what exists actually *and* what exists 'virtually', in God's idea.

Reason

The second kind of knowledge, in which certain aspects of the body are adequately (and therefore truly and certainly) understood. NB, there is no 'faculty of reason'. Reasoning is the activity of the finite mind when it conceives eternal truths.

Transcendent

External. 'X is transcendent to Y' means that X stands outside of Y, and may be different in kind from it. Strictly speaking, there is nothing transcendent, and there are no transcendent causes, in Spinoza's universe. See its opposite, 'immanent'.

'Unconfuse'

To clarify; to transform an inadequate idea into an adequate one.

Unfold

(a) To actualise one's essence. (b) From one adequate idea of some aspect of the body, to deduce a sequence of other adequate ideas.

Universal

A term that the human mind invents to group together many images sharing certain superficial features, e.g. 'animal', 'thing', 'Italian'. All universals are imaginary, based on what appears to the senses, not on the common notions that are truly shared by individuals (IIP40S1).

Further Reading

1. The history of Spinoza's life and thought

If you are interested in Spinoza's life, Nadler (1999) is the place to start. Nadler (2001) explicitly investigates Spinoza's exclusion from the Jewish community. The radical nature of Spinoza's work, its impact on succeeding generations of thinkers, dissenters, and censors throughout Europe, and Spinoza's importance to the Enlightenment, is masterfully treated by Israel (2001). A popular account of Spinoza's encounter with the philosopher G.W. Leibniz is offered in Stewart (2006).

2. Other introductory guides to Spinoza and the *Ethics*

Two books written at introductory level which will introduce you to contemporary debates in Spinoza interpretation and scholarship are Lloyd (1996) and Nadler (2006). Curley (1988) is written for undergraduates and foregrounds scientific questions in the *Ethics*. Deleuze (1988) is an extremely accessible and engaging interpretation of the *Ethics* as practical philosophy. Deleuze focuses on the *Ethics* as a guide for living and thinking, and provides a useful glossary of concepts.

3. Scholarly commentaries and analyses of Spinoza's *Ethics*

As mentioned above, Deleuze (1988) is highly recommended, particularly if you are interested in ethical questions in the *Ethics*. (Deleuze (1990) is a longer and much more challenging text.) If you want to immerse yourself immediately in critical debate, to arm yourself with critical objections to Spinoza, or simply to read an enjoyably devastating philosophical analysis, you cannot do better than Bennett (1984). Older studies often focus on important metaphysical questions that contemporary philosophers no longer find interesting; two that are worth a look are Hallett (1957) and Wolfson (1934). Perhaps the most measured and careful analysis of Spinoza, accessible to the beginner, is Hampshire (1987) (recently republished in Hampshire (2005)). An excellent and wide-ranging collection is the four-volume Lloyd (ed.) (2001). This collection includes essays on law, desire, suicide and the environment, as well as familiar topics in Spinoza's metaphysics, epistemology and ethics.

4. Spinoza beyond philosophy

Recently, a number of books have linked Spinoza's *Ethics* to questions outside philosophy. Damasio (2004) explores how Parts III and IV of the *Ethics* anticipate contemporary developments in neuroscience and the science of the emotions. Gatens and Lloyd (1999), Balibar (1998) and Negri (1991) all consider the applicability of Spinoza's philosophy to contemporary political problems and questions of national identity. De Jonge (2004) is an extended study of Spinoza's relevance to environmental ethics. Goldstein (2006) assesses Spinoza's importance for contemporary Jewish studies. Norris (1991) considers Spinoza's influence on a number of forms of literary and critical theory, including Marxism and deconstruction.

Types of Question You Will Encounter

There are three broad 'genres' of essay question that you are likely to encounter when studying Spinoza at university.

- **Historical**: these questions concern Spinoza's work in its historical or philosophical context. For instance: 'Why does Spinoza appeal to the "state of nature" in Part IV?' 'Compare Spinoza's account of the mind–body relation to that of Descartes'. Answering these questions requires you to consider how Spinoza's arguments, in the *Ethics* and other texts, relate to religious, political and philosophical movements of the seventeenth century (or other times). You may need to refer to historical studies and the work of other philosophers, as well as critical commentaries on Spinoza.
- **Textual**: in these questions you are asked to explain, discuss and/or assess a passage, argument or problem internal to the *Ethics*. For example: 'Explain and assess Spinoza's argument for the existence of God'; 'Are modes the effects of substance, or properties inhering in substance?' 'How is evil related to falsity, on Spinoza's account?' Your answers to these questions should be based largely on your understanding, explanation and critical consideration of Spinoza's *Ethics* itself. You may choose to consult secondary literature to gain additional critical perspectives.

- **Problem-based**: these questions ask you to consider Spinoza's arguments in relation to philosophical problems not specific to Spinoza (e.g. 'Is freedom compatible with determinism? Discuss, with reference to Spinoza'). Sometimes you may be asked to evaluate Spinoza's arguments using terms and methods external to Spinoza's texts ('Is Spinoza a moral relativist?' 'Evaluate Spinoza's philosophy of mind in light of contemporary cognitive science'). In these essays, you will need to refer to critical commentaries to get some background on the problems in question, as well as thinking carefully about Spinoza's *Ethics* itself.

Tips for Writing about Spinoza

Here are some tips for writing your essay on Spinoza.

- Pay attention to the verb used in the essay question. If you are asked to 'explain' a passage, you need to state clearly what you believe Spinoza is saying, and carefully set out, in your own words, how he argues for it. Most essays include an element of exposition: the part of an essay that is dedicated to explaining the text (or a passage of it). If you are assigned to write an 'exposition', you are being asked to write a piece explaining Spinoza's argument (check with your lecturer whether you are also expected to summarise other interpretations of the *Ethics* or explain it in context). If you are asked to 'discuss', 'critically assess' or 'evaluate', you are being asked to consider the material critically and arrive at some conclusion about it. You may be expected to state whether you find Spinoza's argument convincing, and why or why not. You may also be expected to demonstrate your familiarity with a range of critical responses from the secondary literature.
- Whatever type of question you answer, your essay should have a clear argumentative structure. Start with a 'thesis statement' (a statement of the point you are arguing for). Do not just say, 'In this essay I will explain Spinoza's parallelism and then consider some problems with it'. State your position clearly: 'In this essay, I will argue that while Spinoza puts forward a strong

argument for parallelism, it does not stand up to criticism'. Even if you are writing an exposition, you need a thesis statement (e.g., 'In this essay, I will show that Spinoza demonstrates that God's existence is eternal, infinite, and necessary').

- In developing your essay, you should make extensive use of the *Ethics* – it is your primary text. You may need to read a series of propositions many times, take notes, read them again, consult a secondary text, read them again, and then write about them in your own words. Give yourself enough time to work out a really clear and accurate exposition; explaining Spinoza is more difficult than you may think. Do not attempt to critically evaluate Spinoza before you have worked out your exposition of the relevant material from the *Ethics*.

- When you come to critically assess the *Ethics*, adopt a principle of interpretive generosity. Do not assume that Spinoza must be wrong because his ideas are old, unfamiliar or do not seem to meet with your experience. Try to understand the text on its own terms and evaluate it according to its philosophical merits. (You may not accept that sewing machines can think, but does Spinoza offer a good argument for believing that they do? Is that belief necessary to upholding his parallelism?) If you feel that something is wrong or unconvincing, read carefully to see whether Spinoza addresses your problem elsewhere in the text. Spinoza's letters contain many of his responses to objections, and you may find your own objection treated there.

- Avoid making generalisations like 'Spinoza was a rationalist who believed that experience was worthless' or 'as a man of the seventeenth century, Spinoza has no place in his philosophy for women'. Generalisations are usually false and always irritating to lecturers. Such statements cover over the specificities of Spinoza's thought and suggest that you have not thought about it very carefully.

- Use Spinoza's terminology with care. Do not use 'idea' if you mean 'image'; words like 'virtue', 'free' and 'cause' cannot be used casually in an essay on Spinoza. Thinking carefully about words will help you to write more clearly.

- Be careful, too, when using examples. Examples are extremely useful in clarifying a point or illustrating an argument (I have used them throughout this book). But don't allow examples to take over your essay, and definitely don't base your argument on them. An example should provide support for your philosophical point, not take its place.

- When you quote or refer to Spinoza's *Ethics*, make use of the standard referencing system outlined in the Introduction to this book.
- Finally, try to include some original thinking in your essay. Most lecturers do not want to read just a faithful summary of Spinoza and the secondary literature; they want to see evidence that you can think about it and express your own position. That is not, of course, a licence to drop in your personal beliefs or feelings about Spinoza (save that for the course discussion board). But you can, and should, incorporate your own well-considered views about the text or problem you are writing on: explain what your view is, and why you think it is justified. Spinoza, the advocate of building your own reason, would expect nothing less.

Bibliography

Works by Spinoza

Spinoza, Benedictus de (1994), *A Spinoza Reader*, ed. and trans. E. Curley, Princeton, NJ: Princeton University Press.

Spinoza, Benedictus de (2002), *Complete Works*, trans. S. Shirley, ed. M. L. Morgan, Indianapolis, IN: Hackett.

Other Sources

Allison, Henry (1987), *Benedict de Spinoza: an Introduction*, New Haven, CT: Yale University Press.

Balibar, Etienne (1998), *Spinoza and Politics*, trans. P. Snowdon, London: Verso.

Barbone, Steven (1993), 'Virtue and Sociality in Spinoza', *Iyyan, The Jerusalem Philosophical Quarterly* 42, pp. 383–95.

Barbone, Steven (2002), 'What counts as an individual for Spinoza?' in O. Koistinen and J. Biro (eds), *Spinoza: Metaphysical Themes*, Oxford: Oxford University Press, pp. 89–112.

Barbone, Steven and Lee Rice (2001), 'Spinoza and the problem of suicide', in G. Lloyd (ed.), *Spinoza: Critical Assessments*, vol. II, London: Routledge, pp. 262–78.

Bennett, Jonathan (1984), *A Study of Spinoza's Ethics*, Indianapolis, IN: Hackett.

Blom, Hans (2001), 'Politics, virtue, and political science: an interpretation of Spinoza's political philosophy', in G. Lloyd (ed.), *Spinoza: Critical Assessments*, vol. III, London: Routledge, pp. 3–19.

Byrne, Laura (1994), 'Reason and emotion in Spinoza's *Ethics*: the two infinities', in G. Hunter (ed.), *Spinoza: The Enduring Questions*, Toronto: University of Toronto Press, pp. 113–25.

Carr, Spencer (1978), 'Spinoza's distinction between rational and intuitive knowledge', *Philosophical Review* 87, pp. 241–52.

Cottingham, John G. (2001), 'The intellect, the will, and the passions: Spinoza's critique of Descartes', in G. Lloyd (ed.), *Spinoza: Critical Assessments*, vol. II, London: Routledge, pp. 219–38.

Curley, Edwin (1969), *Spinoza's Metaphysics: An Essay in Interpretation*, Cambridge, MA: Harvard University Press.

Curley, Edwin (1973), 'Spinoza's moral philosophy', in M. Grene (ed.), *Spinoza: A Collection of Critical Essays*, Notre Dame, IN: University of Notre Dame Press, pp. 354–76.

Curley, Edwin (1988), *Behind the Geometrical Method: A Reading of Spinoza's Ethics*, Princeton, NJ: Princeton University Press.

Damasio, Antonio (2004), *Looking for Spinoza: Joy, Sorrow, and the Feeling Brain*, London: Vintage.

De Dijn, Herman (2001), 'Naturalism, freedom and *Ethics* in Spinoza', in G. Lloyd (ed.), *Spinoza: Critical Assessments*, vol. II, London: Routledge, pp. 332–48.

De Jonge, Eccy (2004), *Spinoza and Deep Ecology*, Aldershot: Ashgate.

Delahunty, R. J. (1985), *Spinoza*, London: Routledge & Kegan Paul.

Deleuze, Gilles (1988), *Spinoza: Practical Philosophy*, trans. R. Hurley, San Francisco: City Lights.

Deleuze, Gilles (1990), *Expressionism in Philosophy: Spinoza*, trans. M. Joughin, New York: Zone Books.

Della Rocca, Michael (1996a), *Representation and the Mind–Body Problem in Spinoza*, Oxford: Oxford University Press.

Della Rocca, Michael (1996b), 'Spinoza's metaphysical psychology', in D. Garrett (ed.), *The Cambridge Companion to Spinoza*, Cambridge: Cambridge University Press, pp. 192–266.

Della Rocca, Michael (2004), 'Egoism and the imitation of affects in Spinoza', in Y. Yovel and G. Segal (eds), *Spinoza on Reason and the Free Man*, New York: Little Room Press, pp. 123–48.

Descartes, René (1988), *Selected Philosophical Writings*, trans. J. Cottingham, et al., Cambridge: Cambridge University Press.

Deveaux, Sherry (2007), *The Role of God in Spinoza's Metaphysics*, London: Continuum.

Donagan, Alan (1979), 'Spinoza's proof of immortality', in M. Grene (ed.), *Spinoza: A Collection of Critical Essays*, Notre Dame, IN: University of Notre Dame Press, pp. 241–58.

Donagan, Alan (1988), *Spinoza*, London: Harvester Wheatsheaf.

Donagan, Alan (2001), 'Essence and the distinction of attributes in Spinoza's metaphysics', in G. Lloyd (ed.), *Spinoza: Critical Assessments*, vol. II, London: Routledge, pp. 52–67.

Gabbey, Alan (1996), 'Spinoza's natural science and methodology', in D. Garrett (ed.), *The Cambridge Companion to Spinoza*, Cambridge: Cambridge University Press, pp. 142–91.

Garber, Daniel, and Michael Ayers (eds) (1998), *The Cambridge History of Seventeenth-Century Philosophy*, 2 vols., Cambridge: Cambridge University Press.

Garrett, Aaron V. (2003), *Meaning in Spinoza's Method*, Cambridge: Cambridge University Press.

Garrett, Don (1996a), 'Spinoza's Ethical Theory', in D. Garrett (ed.), *The Cambridge Companion to Spinoza*, Cambridge: Cambridge University Press, pp. 267–314.

Garrett, Don (ed.) (1996b), *The Cambridge Companion to Spinoza*, Cambridge: Cambridge University Press.

Garrett, Don (2002), 'Spinoza's *conatus* argument', in O. Koistinen and J. Biro (eds), *Spinoza: Metaphysical Themes*, Oxford: Oxford University Press, pp. 127–58.

Gatens, Moira (2001), 'Spinoza, law, and responsibility', in G. Lloyd (ed.), *Spinoza: Critical Assessments*, vol. III, London: Routledge, pp. 225–44.

Gatens, Moira and Genevieve Lloyd (eds) (1999), *Collective Imaginings: Spinoza, Past and Present*, London: Routledge.

Giancontti, Emilia (2002), 'On the problem of infinite modes', in G. Segal and Y. Yovel (eds), *Spinoza*, Aldershot: Ashgate, pp. 61–82.

Goldstein, Rebecca (2006), *Betraying Spinoza: the Renegade Jew who gave us Modernity*, New York: Nextbook.

Grene, Marjorie (ed.) (1979), *Spinoza: A Collection of Critical Essays*, Notre Dame, IN: University of Notre Dame Press.

Grene, Marjorie and D. Nails (eds) (1986), *Spinoza and the Sciences*, Dordrecht: D. Reidel.

Hallett, H. F. (1957), *Benedict de Spinoza: The Elements of his Philosophy*, London: Athlone.

Hampshire, Stuart (1987), *Spinoza*, Harmondsworth: Penguin.

Hampshire, Stuart (2005), *Spinoza and Spinozism*, Oxford: Oxford University Press.

Harris, Errol E. (1995), *The Substance of Spinoza*, Atlantic Highlands, NJ: Humanities Press.

Hobbes, Thomas (1968), *Leviathan*, Harmondsworth: Penguin.

Hunter, Graeme (ed.) (1994), *Spinoza: The Enduring Questions*, Toronto: University of Toronto Press.

Israel, Jonathan (2001), *Radical Enlightenment: Philosophy and the Making of Modernity 1650–1750*, Oxford: Oxford University Press.

Jarrett, Charles (2002), 'Spinoza on the relativity of good and evil', in O. Koistinen and J. Biro (eds), *Spinoza: Metaphysical Themes*, Oxford: Oxford University Press, pp. 159–81.

Koistinen, Olli and John Biro (eds) (2002), *Spinoza: Metaphysical Themes*, Oxford: Oxford University Press.

Lloyd, Genevieve (1994), *Part of Nature: Self-Knowledge in Spinoza's Ethics*, Ithaca, NY: Cornell University Press.

Lloyd, Genevieve (1996), *Spinoza and the Ethics*, London: Routledge.

Lloyd, Genevieve (2001a), 'Spinoza's environmental ethics', in G. Lloyd (ed.), *Spinoza: Critical Assessments*, vol. IV, pp. 326–43.

Lloyd, Genevieve (ed.) (2001b), *Spinoza: Critical Assessments*, 4 vols. London: Routledge.

Mason, Richard (1997), *The God of Spinoza*, Cambridge: Cambridge University Press.

Matson, Wallace (2001), 'Death and destruction in Spinoza's *Ethics*', in G. Lloyd (ed.), *Spinoza: Critical Assessments*, vol. II, pp. 249–61.

Merleau-Ponty, Maurice (2002), *Phenomenology of Perception*, trans. C. Smith, London: Routledge.

Montag, Warren and Ted Stolze (eds) (1997), *The New Spinoza*, Minneapolis, NY: University of Minnesota Press.

Morrison, James C. (1994), 'Spinoza on the self, personal identity, and immortality', in G. Hunter (ed.), *Spinoza: The Enduring Questions*, Toronto: University of Toronto Press, pp. 31–47.

Nadler, Steven (1999), *Spinoza: a Life*, Cambridge: Cambridge University Press.

Nadler, Steven (2001), *Spinoza's Heresy: Immortality and the Jewish Mind*, Oxford: Clarendon Press.

Nadler, Steven (2006), *Spinoza's Ethics: An Introduction*, Cambridge: Cambridge University Press.

Negri, Antonio (1991), *The Savage Anomaly*, trans. M. Hardt, Minneapolis, MN: University of Minnesota Press.

Nietzsche, Friedrich (1994), *On the Genealogy of Morality*, ed. K. Ansell-Pearson, trans. C. Diethe, Cambridge: Cambridge University Press.

Nietzsche, Friedrich (2001), *The Gay Science*, ed. B. Williams, trans. J. Nauckhoff, Cambridge: Cambridge University Press.

Norris, Christopher (1991), *Spinoza and the Origins of Modern Critical Theory*, Oxford: Blackwell.

Oksenberg Rorty, Amelie (2001), 'Spinoza on the pathos of idolatrous love and the hilarity of true love', in G. Lloyd (ed.), *Spinoza: Critical Assessments*, vol. II, London: Routledge, pp. 293–310.

Parkinson, G. H. R. (1964), *Spinoza's Theory of Knowledge*, Oxford: Oxford University Press.

Ravven, Heidi M. (2001), 'Spinoza's materialist ethics: the education of desire', in G. Lloyd (ed.), *Spinoza: Critical Assessments*, vol. II, London: Routledge, pp. 311–31.

Savan, David (2001), 'Spinoza on duration, time, and eternity', in G. Lloyd (ed.), *Spinoza: Critical Assessments*, vol. II, London: Routledge, pp. 364–90.

Scruton, Roger (2002), *Spinoza: a Very Short Introduction*, Oxford: Oxford University Press.

Segal, Gideon and Yirmiyahu Yovel (eds) (2002), *Spinoza*, Aldershot: Ashgate.

Smith, Steven B. (2003), *Spinoza's Book of Life: Freedom and Redemption in the Ethics*, New Haven, CT: Yale University Press.

Steinberg, Diane (1984), 'Spinoza's ethical doctrine and the unity of human nature', *Journal of the History of Philosophy* 22, pp. 303–24.

Steinberg, Diane (1993), 'Spinoza, method, and doubt', *History of Philosophy Quarterly* 10, pp. 211–24.

Stewart, Matthew (2006), *The Courtier and the Heretic: the Secret Encounter Between Spinoza and Leibniz that Defines the Modern World*, London: Yale University Press.

Wilson, Margaret (2001), 'Objects, ideas, and "minds": comments on Spinoza's theory of mind', in G. Lloyd (ed.), *Spinoza: Critical Assessments*, vol. II, London: Routledge, pp. 97–113.

Wolfson, Harry (1934), *The Philosophy of Spinoza*, 2 vols, Cambridge, MA: Harvard University Press.

Yovel, Yirmiyahu (1989), *Spinoza and Other Heretics*, 2 vols, Princeton, NJ: Princeton University Press.

Yovel, Yirmiyahu (ed.) (1991), *God and Nature: Spinoza's Metaphysics*, Leiden: Brill.

Yovel, Yirmiyahu (ed.) (1994), *Spinoza on Knowledge and the Human Mind*, Leiden: Brill.

Yovel, Yirmiyahu (ed.) (1999), *Desire and Affect: Spinoza as Psychologist*, New York: Little Room Press.

Yovel, Yirmiyahu and Gideon Segal (eds) (1999), *Spinoza on Reason and the Free Man*, New York: Little Room Press.

Zac, Sylvain (2001), 'Life in the philosophy of Spinoza', in G. Lloyd (ed.), *Spinoza: Critical Assessments*, vol. II, London: Routledge, pp. 239–48.

Index